"This book changed my life, and it can change yours, too. Joe Romm understands the secrets of persuasion and messaging and he has distilled them into this must-read book."

Van Jones, President, Rebuild the Dream.

LANGUAGE INTELLIGENCE

LESSONS ON PERSUASION FROM
JESUS, SHAKESPEARE, LINCOLN, AND LADY GAGA

JOSEPH J. ROMM

To Antonia

TABLE OF CONTENTS

INTRODUCTION

*Of all the talents bestowed upon men, none is so
precious as the gift of oratory. He who enjoys it wields
a power more durable than that of a great king. . . .
The subtle art of combining the various elements that
separately mean nothing and collectively mean so
much in an harmonious proportion is known to very
few. . . . [T]he student of rhetoric may indulge the
hope that Nature will finally yield to observation and
perseverance, the key to the hearts of men.*

— Winston Churchill, "The Scaffolding of Rhetoric"[1]

This book will change the way you speak *and* listen. It
will tune up your tweets and build up your blog. My
goal is to help you become more persuasive, more
memorable, and harder to manipulate—help you boost
your language intelligence. You will learn the secrets of
rhetoric, the twenty-five-century-old art of persuasion,
whose masters include Jesus, Shakespeare, the King
James Bible's translators, Abraham Lincoln, Winston
Churchill, Martin Luther King, Bill Clinton, and
modern song writers from Bob Dylan to Lady Gaga.[2]

In the hands of its greatest practitioners, rhetoric has changed the world. As John F. Kennedy said of Churchill, "He mobilized the English language and sent it into battle" to see England through to victory in World War II. In a famous 1858 speech, Lincoln paraphrased Jesus, saying, "A house divided against itself cannot stand," and he extended the house metaphor throughout the speech. His law partner, William Herndon, later wrote that Lincoln had told him he wanted to use "some universally known figure [of speech] expressed in simple language . . . that may strike home to the minds of men in order to raise them up to the peril of the times."[3]

Barack Obama rarely uses these strategies, especially since he became president, a key reason some of his greatest victories, like healthcare reform, turned from milestones into millstones. With no simple message, no natural narrative for his presidency, he has allowed others to define him and his policies, which contributed to the harsh rebuke by voters at the 2010 midterm elections. Fortunately for Obama, presidential elections are graded on a curve, and he only needs to have superior language intelligence to his opponent, Mitt Romney, one of the worst communicators to win any party's presidential nomination in recent memory. In a close election, superior language intelligence becomes even more vital.

Rhetoric is the art of influencing both the hearts and minds of listeners, codified by sages such as

Introduction

Aristotle and Cicero, then raised to high art in England during the reigns of Queen Elizabeth and King James. It has largely fallen into neglect or ridicule and is practiced knowingly by only a select few. What Dante called "the sweetest of all the other sciences," what Lincoln and Churchill so successfully mastered and marshaled to motivate millions in perilous times, is taught hardly anywhere today, although millions of people regularly study its most compelling textbooks: the King James Bible and the works of Shakespeare.[4]

If the Bible is the word of God, then rhetoric is God's way of speaking. The Elizabethans certainly viewed rhetoric that way. One best-selling sixteenth-century handbook asserted that rhetoric makes the orator "the emperour of men's minds & affections, and next to the omnipotent God in the power of persuasion."[5]

Those well-schooled in the Bible are thus well-schooled in rhetoric. Similarly, every great songwriter—our modern bards—inevitably masters rhetoric since rhetoric itself came from the oral tradition of the great bards like Homer. The most popular songs are rhetoric put to music, as we will see by examining hits by Bob Dylan, Elton John, and Lady Gaga, the first musician in history to reach one billion views on YouTube.

Rhetoric is the art of being pithy and profound. In this world of information overload, you have to capture people's attention. In this media menagerie, you have to stand out like a peacock. So this book will help you "wow" people with words—grab them with the most eye-popping headlines, the catchiest catch-phrases, and the sweetest tweets.

Once people are paying attention, you can win them over through what I call "language intelligence." It is the ability to convince people of something by moving them both intellectually *and* emotionally, at both a conscious and unconscious level. Is all this teachable? Absolutely. It was taught for centuries. It was taught to Shakespeare from an early age—and to the translators of the King James Bible, which explains how a committee of four dozen men working in six teams wrote that masterpiece as if with one voice.

Anyone can gain command of the key principles and techniques through study and practice, enhancing the natural language abilities we are all born with. Studying rhetoric would benefit everyone: tweeters, bloggers, lawyers, politicians, managers, writers and songwriters, teachers, public speakers of all kinds—anyone who must make a persuasive case to customers, clients, coworkers, bosses, voters, friends, or lovers—and all of us who might want to resist them.

Chapter One examines how the system of rhetoric has evolved over the past twenty-five hundred years, and why it remains relevant today. The figures of speech have become a vital part of modern advertising. For better or worse, mastery of the figures will grow only more important in a world where everyone is scrambling to stand out by advertising themselves as outstanding.

Introduction

Chapter Two debunks a popular myth that rhetoric equals big words. In fact, "the shorter words of a language are usually the more ancient," as Churchill explained. "Their meaning is more ingrained in the national character and they appeal with greater force." Short words linger with us in great speeches and great slogans, from "To be or not to be" to "Be all that you can be," from "I have a dream" to "Just do it," from "Judge not that ye be not judged" to "Don't ask, don't tell." Short words win.

Chapter Three explores the essential element of all persuasion: repetition, repetition, repetition. Repetition is the primary strategy of society's true masters at getting what they want—children. But it's also how politicians get what they want. As the GOP's master wordmeister, Frank Luntz, explained, "There's a simple rule: You say it again, and you say it again, and you say it again, and you say it again, and you say it again, and then again and again and again and again, and about the time that you're absolutely sick of saying it is about the time that your target audience has heard it for the first time." Repetition is so important to rhetoric that there are some four dozen figures of speech describing different kinds of repetition, ranging from simple alliteration ("compassionate conservative") to complex chiasmus ("Ask not what your country can do for you—ask what you can do for your country"). If you don't repeat, you can't compete.

Joseph J Romm

Chapter Four examines irony from Shakespeare to Seinfeld and *eirons* (who feign ignorance) from Socrates to George W. Bush. Irony is a defining characteristic of the greatest stories, of American popular culture, and of the great political orators. Marc Antony's "Friends, Romans, countrymen" speech in Shakespeare's *Julius Caesar* is, by itself, a master class in irony. As we'll see, Abraham Lincoln, who learned rhetoric in part by studying Shakespearean orations, used the same rhetorical strategy as Antony—ironic repetition—in his crowd-pleasing and career-making Cooper Union speech.

Chapter Five looks at foreshadowing. The best speeches create anticipation before fulfilling the listener's desire: Tell them what you are going to tell them. Perhaps the greatest example can be found in Martin Luther King's 1963 "I have a dream" speech. In the literal shadow of the Lincoln monument, King turns Lincoln's Gettysburg Address into a symbolic foreshadowing of his own remarks one hundred years later.

Chapter Six targets metaphorical missiles and mine fields. Artistotle believed, "The greatest thing by far is to be a master of metaphor." Modern social science research confirms the wisdom of Plato's student: "Studies reveal that *virtually all of our abstract conceptualization and reasoning is structured by metaphor.*" A single, well-crafted metaphor, like a well-crafted building, can endure for ages, as when Churchill

Introduction

said in 1946, "an *iron curtain* has descended across the Continent."

Chapter Seven examines extended metaphor, my favorite figure and the key to framing a picture-perfect speech, song, or political victory. The Gettysburg Address may be the greatest extended metaphor in the English language, with Lincoln turning the bloody battle into a symbolic national crucifixion, although that facet of the speech is rarely taught. The best-selling song of all time, Elton John's "Candle in the Wind," is an extended metaphor as are "Poker Face" and "Bad Romance"—monster hits by Lady Gaga that have been viewed online half a billion times! Winning political campaigns use extended metaphors to define their opponents.

Lastly, rhetoric has a dark side: It can manipulate and mislead. So Chapter Eight uncovers the figures of seduction—devious devices used by popular presidents, sneaky salesmen, crafty Casanovas, and sexy songstresses as well as Shakespeare's Iago and Marc Antony. The language intelligence needed to thwart those ultra-subtle seducers comes naturally to very few. To be resisted and debunked, their verbal tricks must be made explicit, which is my goal here.

I communicate primarily online through the blog I founded in 2006, ClimateProgress.org, a project of the Center for American Progress Action Fund. *Time* magazine named it one of the "Best Blogs of 2010." *Nature* called it "perhaps the world's most influential political climate-change blog." Columnist Tom Friedman called it the "indispensible blog." *U.S. News & World Report* wrote, "In terms of his cachet in the blogosphere, Joe Romm is something like the climate change equivalent of economist (and *New York Times* columnist) Paul Krugman." This success comes at least partly from using the figures.

Online communicators can clearly benefit from an understanding of rhetoric. I think most bloggers would be more effective if they wrote more conversationally. I dictate all of my blog posts (and books) using voice dictation software, which helps my writing match my speaking.

I've come to realize that the single most important part of any blog post is the headline. Newspaper readers read 56 percent of the headlines, but only 13 percent of the stories are at least half-read.[6] Headlines are even more important online since they are what show up in Google searches and tweets. If you can't wow people with your headline, you won't win them with your ideas.

One way to write a wowing headline is to use a figure of speech. The same goes for a memorable tweet. I send out all of my headlines as tweets (along with the link for my blog post). Indeed, I think of them as tweets, a strategy that has already earned ClimateProgress.org some thirty thousand Twitter followers. A key goal of any headline is to get retweeted dozens of times. The best get retweeted hundreds of times and are seen by over a hundred thousand people.

Introduction

Yes, winning headlines must match your well-written story or blog post—otherwise readers won't keep coming back. But if you don't wow them first, they won't ever read the story.

I began studying rhetoric more than two decades ago to become a better writer and speaker and to better understand Shakespeare. While Shakespeare seems cryptic to us today, the 'code' he used was rhetoric, which was far from cryptic to Elizabethans. They were as intensively schooled in it as he was, ten hours a day, six days a week, thirty-six weeks a year. So it was the language he could use to communicate meaning to them rapidly and eloquently.

Shakespeare and his audience knew and used over two hundred figures of speech. The figures—the catalog of the different, effective ways that we talk—turn out to "constitute basic schemes by which people conceptualize their experience and the external world," as one psychologist put it.[7] We think in figures, and so the figures can be used to change the way we think. Audiences remember and are moved when speakers repeat words and phrases, when they use metaphors and irony, and so on.

The figures of speech pervade modern political campaigns, advertising, and popular music, which is why I'll use examples from all those areas. The figures have their greatest power when used "collectively . . . in an harmonious proportion," explained a precocious and prescient twenty-two-year-old Winston Churchill. He had it exactly right—rhetoric is a system. If you want to be persuasive, you, too, will need command of many figures of speech, not just one or two.

Conservatives have adopted messaging strategies that allowed them to succeed politically even with policies that don't have strong popular support. Indeed, that is one reason they turned the tide against President Obama in 2010—simple, relentless messaging.

Similarly, those who deny the reality of climate science have made use of the best rhetorical techniques. Those seeking to inform the public about the very real dangers of a warming climate will need to learn the lessons of the best communicators if they are to overcome the most well-funded disinformation campaign in history.

To sum up, rhetoric is the art of persuasion through the systematic use of the figures of speech. The figures are the grammar of language intelligence. They must be mastered by all who seek to be compelling speakers and writers. Here's how.

CHAPTER ONE

AN EDUCATION IN ELOQUENCE

Rhetoric is "the art of winning the soul by discourse."

—Plato[8]

The figures of speech are the key tools for wowing people into paying attention and then winning them over once they are. That's never been more important than it is today.

Tina Brown, the editor of *The Daily Beast* website, and former editor of *Vanity Fair* and *The New Yorker*, described the challenge of capturing readers as she took over the ailing *Newsweek* magazine: "You have to basically make the assumption that they have absolutely no interest in you whatsoever. There is so little attention to spare, you have to make sure that where their window of attention is open, you're in."[9] Getting noticed and getting "in" have been the twin tasks of rhetoric for over two thousand years.

Humans had learned effective ways to use words long before developing a codified system. The *Iliad* and *Odyssey*, dated from around the eighth century BC, are often labeled the earliest great examples of rhetoric, but the Five Books of Moses have at least as strong a claim. Genesis by itself is a complete rhetoric handbook, containing all the figures of speech, as we will see. The very first story of Adam and Eve reveals the dangerous power of speech. The serpent, "more subtle than any other wild creature," beguiles Eve with deceptive language and false promises into eating from the tree of knowledge, leading to banishment from Paradise. Such are the bitter fruits of lack of language intelligence.

In perhaps the first direct account of the awesome positive power of eloquence, Homer has Odysseus speak of "a certain kind of man" with "comeliness on his words." People who look at him "are filled with joy at the sight, and he speaks to them without faltering in winning modesty, and shines among those who are gathered, and people look on him as on a god when he walks in the city." These are the better fruits of language intelligence.[10]

The Greeks found the ways to teach eloquence to everyone. In ancient Athens, all citizens needed to excel at public speaking because every citizen was required by Greek law to speak in his own behalf in court. Since you were not required to write your own speech, some litigants hired a *logographos*, a speechwriter, to prepare their defense. Others studied the basics of speechmaking with a professional rhetorician.

Over time, rhetoric was turned into a set of rules by Greeks like Gorgias, the first great rhetorician, and Aristotle, who wrote *Rhetoric*, the first in-depth study of the art. Romans like Cicero built on their system. "In addition to logical argument, Gorgias recognized the persuasive force of emotion," as one scholar explained. Gorgias "regarded an orator as a *pscyhagogos*, like a poet, a leader of souls through a kind of incantation," and he analyzed the psychological effects of the figures of speech.[11]

Today, the word *rhetoric* conjures up an overly ornate and stylized form of speech, utterly unlike the way real people speak. In short, the term has been stood on its head. The irony, to use a figure of speech, is that from the very beginning, rhetoric teachers aimed to help orators speak more naturally, in a manner that as closely as possible matched the way people actually speak. Here is Aristotle discussing the importance of matching natural speaking:

> Your language will be appropriate if it expresses emotion and character. . . . To express emotion, you'll employ the language of anger in speaking of outrage; the language of disgust and discreet reluctance to utter a word when speaking of impiety or foulness; the language of exultation for a tale of glory. . . . This aptness of language is one thing that makes people believe in the truth of your story.[12]

How does Aristotle teach us to make people trust us? "Aptness of language." He links specific figures of speech with specific emotional states. For instance, he noted that *hyperbole*, extravagant exaggeration, is used by angry men. Today we hear the most extreme hyperbole in the increasingly shrill political shout-fests that have spread like kudzu over cable TV, debasing the word *debate.*

Like all tools invented by humans, rhetoric can be used for evil purposes. Knowledge of rhetoric allows a speaker to fake every emotion and manipulate any listener. In his 1897 essay, Churchill himself candidly conceded: "The direct, though not the admitted, object which the orator has in view is to allay the commonplace influences and critical faculties of his audience, by presenting to their imaginations a series of vivid impressions which are replaced before they can be too closely examined and vanish before they can be assailed."[13]

Let's call the dark side of rhetoric "the art of seduction." Shakespeare gave his master seducers, like Marc Antony in *Julius Caesar* and Iago in *Othello*, the fullest range of rhetorical skills, including the devious devices I am labeling the figures of seduction. Studying rhetoric helps us avoid the traps set by shrewd seducers.

The awesome power of rhetoric in turn helps explain the triumph of poetry and prose in the England of Queen Elizabeth and King James, which gave the world Shakespeare, Francis Bacon, John Donne, Ben

Johnson, and Christopher Marlowe—all born within a dozen years of each other and all heavily schooled in rhetoric, as were all the translators of the King James Bible.

Most of us today are very far from such mastery of language. How far can be seen by examining the extraordinary education of a typical middle-class Elizabethan like William Shakespeare.

TEACHING LANGUAGE INTELLIGENCE

William was born in 1564, the third child (of eventually eight) and eldest son of John Shakespeare and Mary Arden. At the time of his birth, his father was a glover, and possibly a dealer in wool and leather, in Stratford, a town of some fifteen hundred located eighty miles northwest of London. John was socially ambitious and ultimately became mayor of Stratford.

William likely attended the town grammar school from age seven to at least age thirteen.[14] Grammar schools got their name because they taught grammar— Latin grammar. Latin would be studied through literature, especially Roman writers like Cicero and Virgil. After learning grammar and working on Latin translation, students would write essays of their own. All facts would be repeated, memorized, recited, tested, and used over and over. The school day marched on from six in the morning to nine, then breakfast; more school nine-fifteen to eleven, then lunch; school again from one to five, then supper; and yet one more hour, six to seven—nearly ten hours each day of relentless repetition—six days a week, thirty-six weeks a year, for up to six years.[15] The amount of repetition was staggering: Every single hour of instruction required, according to one sixteenth-century schoolmaster, six or more hours of exercises to apply the lesson to both speaking and writing.

Imagine the impact of such schooling on the future writers of literature and drama. Students would memorize huge parts of famous works, such as Ovid's *Metamorphoses.* Much of the curriculum was rhetoric since the Elizabethans saw eloquence as the greatest skill to be acquired and rhetoric as the key to the Bible and literature. The teaching strategy was systematic: "First learn the figures, secondly identify them in whatever you read, thirdly use them yourself."[16] Hour after hour after hour, identifying every figure in Ovid or Cicero, then creating your own versions.

Shakespeare's artistic genius was thus rooted in an education utterly different from ours, an education wholly grounded in a study of rhetoric and the classics, an education he thoroughly mastered. The same is true of the translators of the King James Bible. No surprise, then, that they wrote their masterpiece just a few years after Shakespeare wrote his masterpieces.

In 1604, James directed that the "the best-learned" in Oxford and Cambridge begin a new translation from the original Hebrew and Greek into English. Some four dozen translators of varying Christian religious beliefs were divided into six teams to translate different pieces of the Bible. Then twelve men, two from each subgroup, worked on the whole final work.

That the King James Bible *did* become a textbook of rhetoric will soon be evident: Many of the most famous examples of every figure of speech can be found in its pages. That the Bible *would* be a textbook of rhetoric was ordained, since the translators were every one a university-trained language scholar with a far more extensive formal education in rhetoric than Shakespeare, who, after grammar school, was purely self-taught.

These were some of the most accomplished linguists and rhetoricians of their time. All but one was an ordained minister. Many were great preachers. As one example, the head of the subgroup that translated the first part of the Bible was Lancelot Andrewes, dean of Westminster Abbey, who ultimately mastered an astonishing fifteen languages.[17]

One italicized line from the title page of the first edition in 1611 provides the final clue as to why the King James Bible became one of the greatest works of rhetoric: *Appointed to be read in churches.* The Bible was written to be read aloud. While literacy was spreading in Renaissance England, many, perhaps most, parishioners were still illiterate and were thrilled to *hear* the eloquent word of God. Thus the King James Bible, like the works of Shakespeare, was designed to move us through our ears, not our eyes. The ears are the kingdom of rhetoric.

RHETORIC IN THE TIME OF LINCOLN

Nineteenth-century America lacked the rigorous teaching of the rhetoric of Shakespeare's day, but orators were widely admired, entertaining large audiences—and larger readerships—with speeches that lasted over two hours and that might be printed in a local newspaper, the text often filling the entire front page. This was the golden age of American oratory, the age of Daniel Webster, of Henry Clay, of Stephen Douglas, and of Abraham Lincoln.

In modern times, with multiple media with which to entertain ourselves—television, movies, radio, the Internet, video games, iPods, and iPads—we can hardly imagine what it was like to live at a time when public speeches and debates were a primary form of entertainment. One 1858 audience, after sitting through three hours of Lincoln and Douglas debating, actually went out to hear another speech. Lincoln himself, after his first debate with Douglas that year, headed off to hear another speech.[18]

Lincoln, a master orator, debater, and rhetorician, was the most consciously rhetorical of our presidents. He once incisively attacked an opponent for employing a particular metaphor—using a metaphor of his own: "I wish gentlemen on the other side to understand that the use of degrading figures [of speech] is a game at which they may not find themselves able to take all the winnings."

In Lincoln's day, aspiring preachers, lawyers, and politicians were taught some rhetoric in college, though they would have learned much just from their study of the Bible. Lincoln worked hard to teach himself elocution and grammar. He studied the great speechmakers of his time, like Daniel Webster, as well the great Elizabethan speechmaker, the Bard of Avon. At an early age, he appears to have studied William Scott's *Lessons in Elocution*, which ends with forty-nine speeches from life and art, nineteen from Shakespeare, including a number that he memorized, such as the soliloquy by King Claudius on the guilt he feels for having murdered Hamlet's father. At the age of twenty-three, Lincoln walked six miles to get a copy of Samuel Kirkham's *English Grammar*, which ends with a several-page discussion of the figures of speech.[19]

The one figure of speech discussed in both Kirkham's book (briefly) and Scott's book (with three full pages of examples) is *antithesis*–placing words or ideas in contrast or opposition, such as Lord Chesterfield's quip, "The manner of speaking is as important as the matter," or Shakespeare's, "Cowards die many times before their deaths, The valiant never taste of death but once."[20] This became one of Lincoln's favorite figures, in unforgettable lines such as "the world will little note, nor long remember, what we say here, but it can never forget what they did here" and "with malice toward none, with charity for all."

Lincoln continued his passion for poetry and Shakespeare throughout his entire life. He spent hours reading passages from Shakespeare to his personal secretary, John Hay, and the artist F. B. Carpenter. After seeing one performance of *Henry IV, Part One*, Lincoln debated Hay on the meaning and emphasis of a single phrase of Falstaff's. During the painting of "Signing of the Emancipation Proclamation," Carpenter describes Lincoln reciting Claudius's thirty-six-line speech "from memory, with a feeling and appreciation unsurpassed by anything I ever witnessed upon the stage." [21]

WE NEED A RENEWED EDUCATION IN RHETORIC

Rhetoric is rarely taught anymore today, at least systematically. Middle-school students spend a few days on simple metaphors and similes like "mad as a hatter," and high schoolers get very little more. Rhetoric is hardly taught in universities or law schools either.

Rhetoric is ignored even by language scholars. A few years ago, a number of academics wrote books to celebrate the four hundredth anniversary of the King James Bible. Yet, none of them looked at the figures of speech or had a substantial discussion of rhetoric, even though the Bible may be the greatest single work of rhetoric ever written. One of them, Alister McGrath, a professor of historical theology at Oxford, actually argued that the brilliance of the Bible was "eloquence by accident," that the translators were aiming for accuracy, but achieved literary merit "unintentionally."[22] Quite the contrary. The eloquence of the King James Bible was achieved not by accident, but by rhetoric.

We should study the figures to boost our language intelligence, to become more persuasive, and to understand "Poets, Orators, or the holy Scriptures" as one Elizabethan best-selling author put it. And there is yet another reason to be re-educated in rhetoric today, equally critical. We are bombarded daily by rhetoric and the figures from those who wish to persuade us or manipulate us. It's always a good idea to discover who's pulling your strings and exactly how they're doing it. Even though rhetoric isn't formally taught, two major forces have helped bring the figures roaring back to the forefront: modern advertising and the "rhetorical presidency."

That modern advertising should rediscover rhetoric was predictable: Rhetoric is the art of verbal persuasion, developed over twenty-five centuries. Modern corporations have spent billions trying to hone in on which words will persuade people to trust them and to purchase their products. Their expensive studies have shown that the use of certain figures "leads to more liking for the ad, a more positive brand attitude, and better recall of ad headlines."[23]

Advertising research also finds that for certain figures, such as puns or metaphors, the act of decoding the figure, of figuring it out, "is necessary to produce its positive incremental effects on attitudes and memory." The subtext is as important as the text.

Since the goal of the headline is to both grab attention and be memorable—two key goals of any speechmaker—the widespread use of figures is inevitable. Rhetoric makes selling compelling.

A comprehensive study of more than two thousand print ads found that three-fourths of ad headlines use figures of speech, with the most common being puns ("Nothing runs like a Deere") and figures of repetition, such as alliteration ("Intel Inside"). One study of award-winning headlines "had a panel of creative directors categorize the headlines according to their commonalities and differences." Of the seven categories derived by their judges, "only one of them (news/information) does not have its basis in figures of speech."[24]

Since my blog, ClimateProgress.org, focuses on news and information, along with commentary, many of my top headlines do not use figures, but a disproportionately large number do. At the same time, ClimateProgress.org consistently gets its headlines retweeted as much as or more than blogs or websites with ten to fifty times the traffic. And one reason, I believe, is my use of the figures of speech.

One of the great things about blogging is the instant, quantitative feedback on what works and what doesn't.

An Education In Eloquence

I analyzed headlines from 2011 that were retweeted two hundred and fifty to one thousand times, which, by my estimate, means they were potentially seen by one hundred thousand to four hundred thousand people. A high fraction of these wowing headlines use one or more figures:

- Mother Nature Is Just Getting Warmed Up: June 2011 Heat Records Crushing Cold Records by 13 to 1 [*pun, personification*]
- 'Job-Killing' EPA Regulations for Chesapeake Bay Will Create 35 Times as Many Jobs as Keystone XL Pipeline [*irony*]
- Shale Shocked: "Highly Probable" Fracking Caused U.K. Earthquakes, and It's Linked to Oklahoma Temblors [*alliteration, pun*]
- Breaking News! Energy Efficiency Programs Are Working, Saving Consumers Millions [*sarcasm*]
- It's Not the Heat, It's the Stupidity: Limbaugh Calls Heat Index a Liberal Government Conspiracy [*pun*]
- Exxon Makes Billion-Dollar Bet Climate Change Is Real, Here Now and Going to Get Worse, But Keeps Funding Deniers [*irony*]
- NASA: It Rained So Hard the Oceans Fell [*metaphor*]

The key is not to have a purely figurative headline. A pun or clever turn of phrase that does not convey to the reader the essence of the article is a double mistake. First, it misses a crucial opportunity to inform those who read only the headline, a far larger number of people than those who actually read the story. Second, it is unlikely to get many clicks, since who among us has time to waste clicking on ambiguous headlines in the hopes the story is something we will be interested in?

In a webinar for a leading online publication, the headline writer explained that only two out of ten people will click on your headline. She gave the following example of how to improve a headline to get noticed and read. The original headline was "Abbott Ditches Its Drug Business." She changed it to "Amputation May Improve Abbott's Prognosis." The result of this personification (and mini-extended metaphor): In the hour before the change, the headline was clicked on 795 times; in the one hour after the headline rewrite, that more than tripled to 2995.

The winner of Twitter's first-ever Golden Tweet for the most retweeted tweet of 2010 was humorist Stephen Colbert for his BP disaster bon mot, "In honor of oil-soaked birds, 'tweets' are now 'gurgles.'" That combines a pun, sarcasm, and (one form of) personification. The second most retweeted tweet of 2010 was from the rapper Drake: "We always ignore the ones who adore us, and adore the ones who ignore us." That's a classic chiasmus (see Chapter Three).

To write more wowing headlines or tweets, you'll have to use more figures. "It's a Brand-You World," proclaimed *Time* magazine in 2006 in a punning headline. If you want to be noticed and remembered, you'll have to use more figures. Certainly they are key weapons in the arsenal of politicians with a winning brand, the ones whose names we remember.

EVOLUTION OF THE RHETORICAL PRESIDENCY

"Rhetoric may now be . . . the primary means of performing the act of presidential leadership," explained communication professor Roderick Hart in 1987.[25] That same year, government professor Jeffrey Tulis argued in his book, *The Rhetorical Presidency*, "Nothing could be further from the founders' intentions than for presidential power to depend upon the interplay of orator and crowd."[26] Tulis shows that, in fact, starting with George Washington through almost the entire nineteenth century, presidents rarely took their case to the public on any major policy or legislative issue of the day, and the few times they did, they were widely criticized. This did not mean there was no role for presidential eloquence—we will always remember Lincoln's words at Gettysburg, Pennsylvania, in 1863—only that presidents didn't expound on the popular issues of the day to promote their policies.

Witness Lincoln's remarkable admission at Pittsburgh, Pennsylvania, in 1861, on "the present distracted condition of the country":

> It is naturally expected that I should say something upon this subject, but to touch upon it at all would involve an elaborate discussion of a great many questions and circumstances, would require more time than I can at present command, and would perhaps, unnecessar-

ily commit me upon matters which have not yet
fully developed themselves. [Immense cheering
and cries of "Good!" "That's right!"][27]

Can we even imagine a modern president in perilous
times making such a public statement, let alone getting
cheered for it?

Beginning especially with Theodore Roosevelt,
who saw the presidency as a "bully pulpit," and
Woodrow Wilson, who publicly campaigned for the
League of Nations (with little success), this view of
the presidency began to change. Ultimately, Tulis
argues, "The modern mass media has facilitated the
development of the rhetorical presidency by giving
the president the means to communicate directly
and instantaneously to a large national audience,"
and by increasing the importance of "verbal dramatic
performance."[28]

The importance of rhetoric to modern presidents
has only increased in the last two decades. First, more
and more, the techniques of modern advertising and
branding are being applied to campaigns to sell candidates, legislation, even wars. In a moment of candor
one expects only from people on truth serum or their
death beds, White House Chief of Staff Andrew Card
offered this explanation for why the president waited
until after his August 2002 vacation to sell the public
on war with Iraq: "From a marketing point of view, you
don't introduce new products in August."[29]

An Education In Eloquence

In 2005, Republican strategists described Bush's messaging strategy using "marketing and public-relations gurus" and "Bush's campaign-honed techniques of mass repetition, never deviating from the script and using the politics of the fear to build support."[30] Modern marketing techniques, repetition, and emotional appeals are catnip for a modern-day *logographos*, a professional speechwriter, among the only people who consciously try to master rhetoric and the figures these days.

Presidential messaging has its biggest impact on elections, I believe. Its impact on legislation is far from clear.[31] The US Senate in particular is not moved by public opinion. Thanks to the extra-constitutional, anti-democratic filibuster, a mere forty-one senators representing a small minority of the US can now effectively block almost any piece of legislation. Elections, however, are a choice between two people, a decision about whom you believe more and whom you trust more. Influencing that very decision is a major reason rhetoric was created in the first place, which is why language intelligence will always be a key element in presidential elections.

Another reason for the growing power of rhetoric in politics is the shrinking power of the mainstream media—the major TV networks and newspapers. The news media has become more and more focused on personalities and entertainment, more obsessed in presidential elections with polls than policies. At the same time, journalists have themselves become celebrities, promoting their own books and TV specials, even showing up in the movies or on TV sitcoms and dramas playing themselves.

Just as journalism and entertainment have merged, so have journalism and politics. Former political strategists routinely appear as political pundits side by side with journalists. Former Republican consultant Roger Ailes controls an entire network, Fox News.

In 2011, the *Washington Post's* Dana Milbank wrote, "Washington journalists give Americans the impression we have shed our professional detachment and are aspiring to be like the celebrities and power players we cover." Journalists and those they cover have become almost indistinguishable, like the men and the pigs at the end of George Orwell's *Animal Farm*.

Finally, we have the countless scandals that have made the media seem no more credible than the powerful politicians they presume to judge. Journalists have fabricated stories, taken money from the government to push its programs, written glowing comments about speeches they contributed ideas to, and cozied up to sources. "It's hard to know now who, if anyone, in the 'media' has any credibility," *Newsweek*'s Howard Fineman wrote in 2005.[32] Whereas only 16 percent of Americans in June 1985 said they "believe little or nothing of what they read in their daily paper," by June 2004 that figure had risen to a staggering 45 percent. By 2009, 63 percent said the news they get is frequently inaccurate.[33]

An Education In Eloquence

The implications of all this for rhetoric in politics are huge. Talk radio, cable news, and the internet have given politicians opportunities to directly address huge audiences with speeches and taped messages. To paraphrase Homer, people are filled with joy to hear a politician who has mastered the art of appealing both to the heart and mind with words, who is the best at telling persuasive stories. This is the realm of rhetoric.

"Tell them a personal story from your life," says GOP pollster and message guru Frank Luntz, advising Republicans how to address an audience on the environment. In his ironically titled 2002 memo, "Straight Talk," he tells Republicans that "it can be helpful to think of environmental (and other) issues in terms of a 'story.' A compelling story, even if factually inaccurate, can be more emotionally compelling than a dry recitation of the truth."[34] Here, then, is another outcome of the media's loss of credibility: If the media has no ability to cry "foul," then even the most devious rhetorical devices can be used safely.

Memorable storytelling, whether in life or politics, is built around the same figures of speech used by the master storytellers, the ancient bards—metaphor, foreshadowing, irony, and especially extended metaphor, which is what some, like the linguist George Lakoff, call a frame.

Narratives are crucial for governing, and the lack of such a narrative is a key reason that President Obama has been far less successful at communications than many people expected. As columnist Ruth Marcus put it in 2011, "On health care, [Obama] took on a big fight without being able to articulate a clear message."[35]

Rhetoric remains as potent as ever. Let us see how rhetoric is done when rhetoric is done right.

CHAPTER TWO

THE FIRST RULE:
SHORT WORDS WIN

The most ancient English words are of one syllable,
so that the more monosyllables that you use,
the truer Englishman you shall seem.

—George Gascoigne[36]

The big myth about rhetoric is that rhetoric equals big words. If I were to wish but one point to stick with you here, it would be that short words are the best words. Short words win. Short words sell. In an era of snappy sound-bites and sexy slogans, the pitch must be pithy or the channel will be changed.

"There is no more important element in the technique of rhetoric than the continual employment of the best possible word," wrote the young Winston Churchill. With our misconceived modern notions, we dismiss rhetoric as flowery language and fifty-dollar words. But the reverse is true: "The unreflecting often imagine that the effects of oratory are produced by the use of long words," Churchill explained. But "shorter words . . . appeal with greater force."[37]

That is not a modern gloss on rhetoric. It is not even a new idea. The first thing an orator must do is "utter his mind in plain words," according to one best-selling book of Shakespeare's day. The author even quotes Julius Caesar, "Beware as long as thou livest of strange words."[38]

Returning to Churchill, "All the speeches of great English rhetoricians . . . display a uniform preference for short, homely words of common usage." We hear the truth of his advice in the words that linger with us from all of the world's great speeches:

- Judge not that ye be not judged
- To be or not to be
- Lend me your ears
- Four score and seven years ago
- Blood, toil, tears and sweat
- Ask not what your country can do for you
- I have a dream

The genius of Shakespeare is a genius he brought to us through short words. When Lady Macbeth's guilty conscience over the murder of old King Duncan drives her to wash her hands over and over again, and to walk and talk in her sleep, she starts with: "Yet here's a spot," and then "Out, damn't spot! Out, I say! One—two, why then 'tis time to do't." And she ends her speech by saying, "Yet who would have thought the old man to have had so much blood in him?" When Polonius gives his advice to his son Laertes in *Hamlet*, he ends with these words: "This above all: to thine own self be true, and it must follow, as the night the day, thou can not then be false to any man."

The words have power and pathos because they are so short. Shakespeare has distilled his art to its very essence.

Short words stick in our minds, which is why they are found in the phrases we remember, that we pick up and repeat, like the pithy Hebrew idioms that have come into common use through the English of the King James Bible:

to pour out one's heart	a man after his own heart
to lick the dust	under the sun
to fall flat on his face	sour grapes
to stand in awe	from time to time
to put words in his mouth	the skin of my teeth[39]

The power of short words to become the language we love to hear again and again can also be heard in the songs that touch us the most. Those who would have been poets in the past now become bards of pop music. Their best songs are works of art—works of rhetorical art.

Here are the opening lines of "Like a Rolling Stone," the 1965 Bob Dylan ballad voted the greatest rock 'n' roll song of all time: "Once upon a time you dressed so fine, You threw the bums a dime in your prime, didn't you?"[40] Dylan is a master of rhetorical devices, learned from studying the great poets and lyricists. His desire to improve his language intelligence was so great that he regularly visited the New York Public Library's microfilm room to read newspapers from the 1850s and 1860s. Why? As he explains in his autobiography, "I wasn't so much interested in the issues as intrigued by the language and rhetoric of the times."[41]

Dylan repeats the simple phrase "How does it feel" eight times in the song. Why? To do what rhetoric does best—involve us in the song *emotionally*. In the next chapter, we'll see many examples of the repetition of simple words in the most popular songs.

Successful ads, like successful speeches and songs, also use simple words that are repeated. Modern marketers spend billions every year pushing their products. To make sure their messages move us, companies build their advertising campaigns around time-tested tricks based on decades of research.

Here are a few memorable advertising slogans. In every one of them we hear the power of short words to stick in our memories, to become phrases that affect our choices, the products we open our wallets for:

Just Do It	M'm, M'm, Good!
The King of Beers	We bring good things to life
Have it your way	When it rains it pours
Where's the beef?	We love to fly and it shows
Good to the last drop	I'd like to buy the world a Coke

The First Rule: Short Words Win

Be all that you can be   All the news that's fit to print
It's the real thing   No more tears
You can trust your car to the man who wears the star

You can go a long way on short words.

POLITICS AND SHORT WORDS

Politics is where Madison Avenue meets Main Street in a war of words to win the hearts and minds of voters. Again, simple wins.

President Ronald Reagan was called the Great Communicator, even by his political opponents. The root of that greatness was his simple style. In his crucial debate with President Carter in 1980, he decisively defined himself and his style with two memorable phrases made up of simple words that still pack a punch.

In the middle of the debate, Carter attacked Reagan for his position on Medicare. Reagan began his sharp reply, "There you go again," as if he, the challenger, were the wise teacher and Carter the callow youth in need of correction. One commentator later called those words "the beginning of the Reagan presidency."[42]

At the end of the debate, Reagan introduced a key question, a rhetorical question, that has since been repeated by countless candidates. He asked the audience to imagine itself at the polls and about to make the key decision. His words are worth repeating at length to hear just how much you can say with short words repeated often:

> I think when you make that decision, it might be well if you would ask yourself, *are you better off than you were four years ago?* Is it easier for you to go and buy things in the stores than it was four years ago? . . . Do you feel that our security is as safe, that we're as strong as we were four years ago? And if you answer all of those questions yes, why then, I think your choice is very obvious as to whom you will vote for. If you don't agree, if you don't think that this course that we've been on for the last four years is what you would like to see us follow for the next four, then I could suggest another choice that you have. This country doesn't have to be in the shape that it is in.[43]

Carter, who before the debate was close in the polls, lost ground steadily after it and was badly defeated by Reagan. But for this debate, and for Reagan's simple words, the election and world history might have been quite different.

President George W. Bush also liked to keep it simple. Michael Gerson, one of his long-time speech writers, said, "He likes simple declarative sentences."[44] So should we all.

Bush's verbal style was best heard in his most famous off-the-cuff lines, which were delivered at Ground Zero on September 13, 2001, to relief workers, police, and firefighters. Using a bullhorn, he began to deliver un-prepared remarks, but the sound was garbled. A worker shouted, "We can't hear you!" Bush replied: "I can hear you, the rest of the world can hear you, and the people who knocked these buildings down will hear all of us soon." Bush's lines were classic rhetoric, simple words with a lot of repetition.

The Democrats, however, have had a love affair with candidates—from Michael Dukakis to John Kerry—who either cannot speak in simple language naturally or lack the discipline to do so in spite of themselves. *Newsweek* reported in November 2004 that "when speechwriters wrote in pithy lines, Kerry would cross them out," saying, "It sounds so slogany."[45] He had it half right: Pithy lines are slogany, but slogany is what sells.

Simple slogans prevail in politics (and so do people who speak simply): *Speak softly and carry a big stick*; *New Deal*; *It's the economy, stupid*; *No Child Left Behind*. Bill Clinton's administration was always searching for the simple slogans to put on a complex issue: *Don't ask, don't tell*, as a policy for dealing with gays in the military, and *Mend it, don't end it*, as an approach for dealing with affirmative-action. Classic slogans like these—short words combined with figures of speech such as repetition and rhyme—helped Clinton become the first Democrat in sixty years to win two presidential elections.

What could be simpler than Obama's slogan in his winning 2008 campaign: "Yes, we can"?

I blog on climate science, solutions, and politics. I'm a physicist by training and have been critical of scientists for not explaining in clear language how failure to quickly and sharply reduce greenhouse gas emissions threatens human civilization.

Scientists are not known for being great communicators. They are trained in logic, in fact-based argument, and that makes them almost anti-rhetoricians, as we will see.

Like many experts, they tend to use complex jargon, rather than words that can be easily understood by most people. A classic climatologist phrase is "anthropogenic global warming," which could not be more off-putting. The word "anthropogenic" simply means "human-caused" or "man-made." Why not just say so?

A useful exercise for public speakers is to practice your talk using only short words, preferably words of one syllable. No, that won't be your final talk, but you will learn a great deal in the effort.

Simple also works when you write. The first of the six rules George Orwell offered in his 1946 essay, "Politics and the English Language," was, "Never use a long word where a short one will do."

Once an orator has chosen the best and shortest words or slogan, the next step is to say them again and again.

CHAPTER THREE

IF YOU DON'T REPEAT, YOU CAN'T COMPETE

There's a simple rule:
You say it again, and you say it again, and you say
it again, and you say it again, and you say it again,
and then again and again and again and again, and
about the time that you're absolutely sick of saying it is
about the time that your target audience has heard it
for the first time.

—Frank Luntz[46]

Eloquence requires the repetition of words and phrases. Persuasion requires the repetition of slogans, sentences, and ideas.

Beyond its ability to convey meaning, "repetition, the re-experiencing of something identical, is clearly in itself a source of pleasure," as Sigmund Freud wrote.[47] The pleasure we derive from repeated words and phrases begins at an early age.

Who is more repetitious than a small child, starting with the primal words *mama* and *dada* that adults gush over in a frenzy of positive reinforcement? Both words feature the most elemental figure of repetition, *alliteration* (from the Latin for "repeating the same letter").

Can anyone delight more than a small child in a story that is told again and again or a movie that is seen again and again? And we never outgrow our love of repetition. Haven't we all listened to a new record, CD, or digital music file over and over again—or had a jingle play over and over and over in our heads even when we don't think we want to hear it?

And the songs themselves are highly repetitious. Lady Gaga is the first musician in history to hit one billion views on YouTube. Her name itself is elemental repetition—Ga Ga. Her song "Poker Face" has been viewed online over a third of a billion times and was the most popular song of 2009.[48] In that song she repeats the title, "poker face," thirty times. And she repeats the "p" sound—as in the line "P-p-p-poker face, p-p-poker face"—fifty times.

The most watched YouTube video of all time is "Baby," in which teen sensation Justin Bieber repeats the alliterative title an astounding fifty-four times. The video has been viewed some 600 million times—which means the word "baby" has been repeated 30 billion times in total!

The TV shows we watch are studies in repetition: Catch phrases become catchy only by repetition. Here are just a few, from the A's through E's:

If You Don't Repeat, You Can't Compete

Aaaayhh! (The Fonz)
And that's the way it is.
And awa-a-a-y we go!
Baby, you're the greatest!
Beam me up, Scotty.
Be careful out there.
Book 'em, Danno!
Can we talk?[49]

Dee plane! Dee plane!
The devil made me do it.
D'oh!
Don't have a cow, man!
Dy-no-mite!
Eh, what's up, doc?
Exc-u-u-u-se me!

If we didn't like such catch phrases, if they weren't a key to the popularity of TV, then why are there so many? Why does pretty much every hit show have them? And why do we adopt them as our own and repeat them again and again and again?

Then, of course, we have the ads. Not only do the slogans of the last chapter stick with us because they are simple words repeated in ads that are run over and over again, but often the repetition is within a single ad. The Energizer Bunny "keeps going and going and going." Cats sing for their Meow Mix supper: "Meow, Meow, Meow, Meow"—just trying to count how many "meows" in one ad locks the jingle into your brain. And we have the impossible-to-forget AFLAC duck, whose mere mention makes one wince. If it walks like a duck, and talks like a duck, and quacks like a duck, it's probably an ad.

Many studies find that repeated exposure to a statement increases its acceptance as true. In fact, a 2007 study found that hearing one person express an opinion repeatedly leads listeners "to estimate that the opinion is more widespread relative to hearing the same communicator express the same opinion only once." The more you repeat, the more you "sound like a chorus."[50]

Repetition works. Repetition sells. That's why the world's major companies spend their money on repetition.

Simply repeating the same thing over and over again is the top strategy of every master persuader—from small children to large advertisers—and thus is the top strategy of master politicians. Michael Deaver, the Karl Rove of the Reagan presidency, said in 2003 of the Bush White House: "This business of saying the same thing over and over and over again—which to a lot of Washington insiders and pundits is boring—works. That was sort of what we figured out in the Reagan White House. And I think these people do it very, very well."[51]

Former presidential speechwriter James Fallows quotes one advisor to former Texas governor Ann Richards, who was bested by Bush in a 1994 debate, saying that even a decade ago, Bush had "that remarkable ability to stick to his message and repeat it no matter what." In 2005, Bush himself admitted, "In my line of work you got to keep repeating things over and over and over again for the truth to sink in, to kind of catapult the propaganda."[52]

An early 2005 Republican strategy document from Frank Luntz on "An Energy Policy for the 21st Century" argues, "Innovation and 21ˢᵗ Century technology should be at the core of your energy policy" and repeats the word "technology" thirty times. In an April 2005 speech describing his proposed energy policy, President Bush repeated the word "technology" more than forty times, more than once a minute. The magazine *Business Week* noted that "what's most striking about Bush's Apr. 27 speech is how closely it follows the script written by Luntz earlier this year."[53]

The need to fill up a twenty-four-hour news cycle and the ever-growing number of media outlets means the only way to get a message out is to shout it over and over again on every outlet. Much of the public is barely paying attention, including key targets of modern presidential campaigns: the occasional voter and the swing voter. The day after the 2004 election, the cabdriver I rode with said that one of Kerry's biggest blunders was calling terrorism a "nuisance." But Kerry didn't say that—he said he wanted to get to the "place we were, where terrorists are not the focus of our lives but they're a nuisance," words very similar to ones previously used by Brent Scowcroft, national security adviser to Bush's father—but the opposition repeatedly said he said it, and that's what matters most these days.[54]

With the mainstream media more of a town crier or stenographer than an honest broker, and with the rise of new media that allow campaigns to deliver messages unfiltered (and that let consumers take only the slant of news they like), repeated distortions and smears are as effective as repeated truths. Maybe more so—since the distortions can be designed to hit hot buttons, create irony, or ring truer than the truth would, as we will see in later chapters.

Even a non-native speaker like Arnold Schwarzenegger learned the art of selling through repetition, whether selling a movie or selling himself. "You have to do more than just go and have a little press conference," the California governor said in 2005. "So the spectacle, showmanship, selling, promoting, marketing, publicizing, all those things are extremely important." And while he learned the value of endless marketing in Hollywood, in the gym he learned the value of endless repetition: "The more often you do something, the better you get. I come from the world of reps. Remember that. It is all reps."[55]

Shakespeare and his audience knew simple repetition was effective. Consider how Shakespeare's master of rhetorical seduction, Iago in *Othello*, manipulates Roderigo, a Venetian gentleman who desires Desdemona even though she has just eloped with Othello. Iago tells Roderigo that despite the fact Desdemona is now married, he can still win her over if he gives Iago money to buy things to woo her with. Iago then launches into the astonishing repetition of the phrase "*put money in thy purse*" ("sell your assets to raise money"). In fourteen lines he repeats the phrase a half dozen times! A few lines later, Iago and Shakespeare tell us how much they believe in the power of repetition when Iago says, "*I have told thee often, and I re-tell thee again and again.*" Roderigo, as expected, gives in: "I am changed: I'll go sell all my land." It is all reps.

In mid-August of 2004, the dog days of the Kerry campaign, as their missteps mounted and their messages miscued, I asked someone close to John Kerry why the campaign didn't pick one message and keep repeating it. "We hit them on something different every day," came the reply. "Besides, most of America is not paying as much attention right now as they will in October." The logic was backwards. When people aren't paying much attention, the only message that can get through is one that is repeated over and over, again and again.

Why do most Democrats seem worse at this repetition business than most Republicans? At one level, as Will Rogers said more than seventy years ago, "I don't belong to any organized party. I'm a Democrat." To the extent that Democrats see themselves as the party of diversity, the rainbow coalition, they don't like to encourage message discipline.

But there's another way of looking at this. Republicans had become the party of the regular churchgoers, and Bush himself had been famously born-again. Church is one of the few places where rhetoric is glorified and repeated endlessly. Those who read the King James Bible regularly are schooling themselves with the greatest single work of rhetoric ever written.

So it is no accident that a born-again Christian like President Bush might be comfortable repeating his message over and over again. And I think it is no accident that the first Democrat in six decades to get re-elected President was a Southern Baptist, Bill Clinton.

The Gospel according to John opens with this repetitive, alliterative sentence: "In the beginning was the Word, and the Word was with God, and the Word was God." As brilliant as the translators of the King James Bible were, some Greek words are tricky to translate. They used the word "word" here for the original Greek word "logos," which can also be translated as "language" and "speech." Many authorities have noted that the phrase "Word (logos) of God" reveals "God's desire and ability to 'speak' to the human." To the believer, the Bible represents God's most eloquent message to his children. *The Garden of Eloquence*, a best-selling Elizabethan rhetoric text, says that rhetoric makes the orator "next to the omnipotent God in the power of persuasion."[56]

The Bible makes clear that repetition is among the most powerful of persuasion strategies—so powerful, in fact, that it can even convince God Himself to change His mind. In Genesis, God tells Abraham of His plan to destroy Sodom and Gomorrah "because their sin is very grievous," which leads to a remarkable exchange:

And Abraham drew near, and said, "Wilt thou also destroy the righteous with the wicked? Peradventure there be fifty righteous within the city: Wilt thou also destroy and not spare the place for the fifty righteous that are therein? That be far from thee to do after this manner, to slay the righteous with the wicked: And that the righteous should be as the wicked, that be far from thee: Shall not the Judge of all the earth do right?"

And the Lord said, "If I find in Sodom fifty righteous within the city, then I will spare all the place for their sakes."

Most men might have stopped there, knowing they had perhaps saved an entire city with their words—but Abraham was not most men. Indeed, now that he knew the words to persuade God, he pressed his case:

"Peradventure there shall lack five of the fifty righteous: wilt thou destroy all the city for lack of five?" And He said, "If I find there forty and five, I will not destroy it."
And he spake unto him yet again, and said, "Peradventure there shall be forty found there. And He said, I will not do it for forty's sake."
And he said unto him, ". . . Peradventure there shall thirty be found there."
And He said, "I will not do it, if I find thirty there."
And he said, ". . . Peradventure there shall be twenty found there."
And He said, "I will not destroy it for twenty's sake."
And he said, ". . . Peradventure ten shall be found there."
And He said, "I will not destroy it for ten's sake."

Joseph J Romm

This passage teaches us that repetition is an awesome means of persuasion.[57]

I believe one reason true orators, especially those well schooled in the Bible, don't mind repeating slogans or whole sentences is that they have so much practice repeating words and phrases, which is the heart of rhetoric. Certainly Bill Clinton was comfortable with both the Bible and repetition. Consider these words from his July 1992 speech accepting the nomination at the Democratic National Convention in his campaign against George Bush, Sr.:

> Of all the things George Bush has ever said that I disagree with, perhaps the thing that bothers me most is how he derides and degrades the American tradition of seeing and seeking a better future. He mocks it as the "vision thing."
>
> But just remember what the Scripture says: "Where there is no vision, the people perish."
>
> I hope—I hope nobody in this great hall tonight, or in our beloved country has to go through tomorrow without a vision. I hope no one ever tries to raise a child without a vision. I hope nobody ever starts a business or plants a crop in the ground without a vision. For where there is no vision, the people perish.
>
> . . . And so I say again: Where there is no vision, America will perish.

In his 1996 acceptance speech, Clinton created an optimistic image for his second term: "We need to build a

38

bridge to the future. And that is what I commit to you to do. So tonight let us resolve to build that bridge to the twenty-first century." He repeated the bridge metaphor in various forms two dozen times in his remarks.[58]

The speech that brought Barack Obama to national attention, his July 27, 2004, keynote address at the Democratic National Convention, was a textbook of repetition:

> **If there's** a child on the south side of Chicago who can't read, that matters to me, even if it's not my child. **If there's** a senior citizen somewhere who can't pay for her prescription and has to choose between medicine and the rent, that makes my life poorer, even if it's not my grandmother. **If there's** an Arab-American family being rounded up without benefit of an attorney or due process, that threatens my civil liberties. . . .
>
> Yet even as we speak, there are those who are preparing to divide us, the spin masters and negative ad peddlers who embrace the politics of anything goes. Well, I say to them tonight, there's not a liberal **America** and a conservative **America**; there's the United States of **America**. There's not a black America and white **America** and Latino America and Asian **America**; there's the United States of **America**. The pundits like to slice and dice our country into red **states** and blue **states**; red **states** for Republicans, blue **states** for Democrats. But I've got news for them, too. We worship an awesome God in the blue **states**, and we don't like federal agents poking around our libraries in the red

> **states**. We coach Little League in the blue **states**
> and have gay friends in the red **states**. There are
> patriots who opposed the war in Iraq and patri-
> ots who supported it. We are one people, all of us
> pledging allegiance to the stars and stripes, all of
> us defending the United **States** of **America**.

This remains Obama's most memorable speech and his most memorable riff in it. Simple language, with repetition.

On the rare occasions when Obama does simplify his message and forcefully repeat himself, people get the message. His September 2011 speech to promote his American Jobs Act was "probably his most rousing political performance in a long while," according to MSNBC's Chris Matthews. *Huffington Post*'s Howard Fineman wrote, "Obama Puts Passion Into Jobs Speech Rarely Seen In His Presidency."[59]

What was the secret of Obama's passionate and rousing speech? He repeated some variation of the phrase "pass this bill" seventeen times.[60] Simple words, lots of repetition. It isn't rocket science or constitutional law. Obama ended the speech with a classic piece of rhetoric from JFK:

> President Kennedy once said, "Our problems are
> man-made, therefore they can be solved by man.
> And man can be as big as he wants."

Simple words, repeating the key one.

But that jobs speech was an exception, which is why it was noticed. Try to remember the words Obama used

to explain why Americans needed healthcare reform. I doubt you can, but I'm pretty sure you can remember what the opponents of healthcare reform said about it:
- "government takeover of healthcare"
- "government rationing care"
- "No Washington politician or bureaucrat should stand between you and your doctor"

These aren't actually true of the healthcare bill that passed, but they are the poll-tested language that Luntz urged conservatives to repeat over and over again in a memo published online, "The Language of Healthcare 2009."[61] He himself repeats the word "takeover" (Washington or government) a dozen times, and the words "rationing" and "bureaucrat" appear over two dozen times each in the memo.

Luntz practices what he preaches—and conservatives preach what Luntz practices. Repetition works.

THE MANY FIGURES OF REPETITION

Repetition has never gone out of style in great speechmaking to emphasize key words and ideas, to make them stick in the mind. This key goal of repetition has been understood for millennia, hence the Latin expression *Repetitio mater memoriae*, "Repetition is the mother of memory."

Consider one of the most popular figures of repetition: rhyme. Studies suggest that if a phrase or aphorism rhymes then people are more likely to view it as true. People more readily believe "woes unite foes" describes human behavior accurately than they do "woes unite enemies."[62] All these years after the 1995 O. J. Simpson murder case, defense attorney Johnnie Cochran's phrase "If it doesn't fit, you must acquit" still sticks in the mind. It's a powerful mnemonic that hardwires what the jurors saw in the courtroom—when Simpson tried on the bloodstained "murder gloves" they didn't fit—with the verdict Cochran wanted and ultimately won for his client. Even simple repetition remains powerfully persuasive.

Repetition is so important to rhetoric that there are some four dozen figures of speech describing different kinds of repetition. The different figures have different purposes.

Early English rhetoric texts may be half a millennium old, but they still have much to teach us. They provide roadmaps for when and where to use the figures.

For instance, *anaphora* repeats the same words at the beginning of a series of sentences or clauses. The best-selling Elizabethan author John Hoskins notes "this figure beats upon one thing to cause the quicker feeling in the audience." It works brilliantly to rally a nation at war in Churchill's famous 1940 speech: "We shall fight in France, we shall fight on the seas and oceans, we shall fight . . . in the air. . . . We shall fight on the beaches, we shall fight on the landing grounds, we shall fight in the fields and in the streets, we shall fight in the hills. . . ." We can hear these powerful words echo in our heads because Churchill understood that "every speech is a rhymeless, meterless verse."[63]

Here are a few lines from the popular 1915 stump speech of Carrie Chapman Catt, one of the leaders of the US women's suffrage movement:

> *Do you know* that the question of votes for women is one which is commanding the attention of the whole civilized world? . . .
> *Do you know* that the women of New Zealand and the women of Australia possess all the political rights accorded to men?
> *Do you know* that the women of Finland vote in all elections upon the same terms as men? . . .
> *Do you know* that in Norway all women have the full Parliamentary vote? . . .
> *Do you know* that the women of Iceland have the full Parliamentary franchise? . . .[64]

She refines and amplifies this theme with another twenty "Do you know?" rhetorical questions on the same subject.

Because of its rousing nature, because it can "awake a sleepy or dull person," this figure can be found in most of the greatest speeches and preachings, from the Sermon on the Mount—Jesus' speech opens with the phrase, "Blessed are . . ." used nine times in nine consecutive lines—to Martin Luther King's 1963 speech, which repeats again and again the stirring phrases "I have a dream" and "Let freedom ring."

The converse figure is *epistrophe*—when many clauses have the same ending. Hoskins explains, "This figure is rather of narration or instruction than motion." We can hear that in the Gettysburg Address, as Lincoln instructed those present that they must "highly resolve ... that government of the people, by the people, for the people shall not perish from the earth."[65]

To digress (which itself is a figure), we cannot always know if the great speechmakers used a particular figure in a particular situation out of a conscious choice or if they found the figure because of their natural instinct for language. In the case of Lincoln and Churchill, it seems likely the choice was intentional. Lincoln was self-consciously rhetorical. For instance, he not only criticized others for their use of specific figures, he himself was roundly attacked for his use of particular ones.

As for Churchill, how many twenty-two-year-olds have written their own manifesto of rhetoric? And in his autobiographical novel *Savrola*, Churchill wrote of his hero, an eloquent politician: "These impromptu feats of oratory existed only in the minds of the listeners; the flowers of rhetoric were hothouse plants." The garden of eloquence requires close cultivation.

Modern presidents have teams of speechwriters, so it is hard to know what words are theirs. We can look for spontaneous moments, but these are rarer and rarer, and as with Churchill in the last century and TV news today, spontaneity can be scripted.

If You Don't Repeat, You Can't Compete

Some of the most revealing moments come in presidential debates, but many of those moments are no doubt scripted also.

Returning to the figures, not all of the power of repetition can be easily described. After discussing several figures of repetition, the author of one Roman rhetoric text concludes, "There inheres in repetition an elegance which the ear can distinguish more easily than words can explain."

Perhaps the most elegant—and certainly one of the most popular—figures of repetition is *chiasmus*: words repeated in inverse order. Chiasmus is a great source of aphorisms. Mae West famously said, "It's not the men in my life, it's the life in my men." Ray Bradbury advised writers, "You have to know how to accept rejection and reject acceptance."

A chiasmus is perfect for a rejoinder, for turning an insult back on the person who uttered it. In the 2002 movie *Die Another Day*, James Bond (Pierce Brosnan) says to gadget-guru Q (John Cleese), "You're smarter than you look," to which Q replies, "Better than looking smarter than you are."

Chiasmus has proved irresistible to presidents and their speechwriters. In his first inaugural, JFK had two: "Ask not what your country can do for you—ask what you can do for your country," as noted earlier, and "Let us never negotiate out of fear. But let us never fear to negotiate." And we heard it again in President Bush's post-9/11 speech: "Whether we bring our enemies to justice, or bring justice to our enemies, justice will be done." Orators who remember to use chiasmus will be remembered as orators.

Chiasmus makes for a memorable tweet, since it is pithy and profound. The second most retweeted tweet of 2010 was from the rapper Drake: "We always ignore the ones who adore us, and adore the ones who ignore us." No, it's not an original sentiment, but then there are very few truly original thoughts. The trick to wowing people is to say an old truth in a new way.

Chiasmus makes for a wowing headline. *Forbes* posts the web statistics for its articles. One of its most widely read and shared posts of 2012 was a February piece on the debate over legislation on internet piracy headlined, "You Will Never Kill Piracy, and Piracy Will Never Kill You."[66] The article has been viewed an amazing 430,000 times, and the headline was probably viewed by more than ten times as many.

Shakespeare was fond of the figure. In *Twelfth Night* he wrote, "Better a witty fool than a foolish wit." Hamlet offers the following instructions on acting: "Suit the action to the word, the word to the action." Jesus was partial to chiasmus:

- Judge not, that ye be not judged.
- The sabbath was made for man, and not man for the Sabbath.
- Ye have not chosen me, but I have chosen you.

Chiasmus is divine.

If You Don't Repeat, You Can't Compete

Jesus is the master preacher, the master of rhetoric, able to turn his enemies' words against them. When the Pharisees try "to catch him in his words," by asking him whether or not it is "lawful to give tribute to Caesar," he replied with a memorably rhetorical phrase, "Render to Caesar the things that are Caesar's, and to God the things that are God's." And so we have yet another reason to study rhetoric: So that people will not be able to catch you in your own words.

A famous use of repetition as a rejoinder in modern politics occurred during the 1988 vice-presidential debate between Senators Dan Quayle and Lloyd Bentsen. Quayle, a relatively young senator, had repeatedly come under questioning about his experience to take over the presidency should the need arise. Finally, he decided to compare himself to another relatively young senator: "I have as much experience in the Congress as Jack Kennedy did when he sought the presidency." Analogies are always risky—as are their figurative cousins, metaphor and simile (see Chapter Six)—and this one created an opening for a stinging reply: "Senator, I served with Jack Kennedy, I knew Jack Kennedy, Jack Kennedy was a friend of mine. Senator, you are no Jack Kennedy." Here the repetition allowed Bentsen to undercut the original comparison and underscore the experience gap.

An especially important rhetorical device is to repeat a word but use a different sense of the word and/or possibly a different ending, such as a plural or past tense. The most general term for this figure is *ploce*. Lincoln, in the Gettysburg Address, uses *dedicate/ dedicated* six times, and his repetition of that key word is inevitably a major focus of analyses of the speech. He starts by saying our nation was "*dedicated* to the proposition that all men are created equal" and that the civil war is testing whether a nation "so *dedicated* can long endure." He then switches usage to say those present have come to "*dedicate*" part of the battlefield for those who died so the nation might live. But then says, "we cannot *dedicate*, we cannot consecrate" because the soldiers, living and dead, have already done that. Rather, the living must be "*dedicated*" to the unfinished work the soldiers began, "*dedicated* to the great task" of ensuring the survival of this government of the people, by the people, for the people. The drumbeat repetition marches the listener toward the lesson Lincoln wants to leave them with, a dedication to the survival of democracy in America.

Two final points. First, while simple repetition is a crucial element of persuasion, of "wowing" people, it can't succeed by itself forever. That's clear from the swift rise and fall of one-time GOP presidential candidate Herman Cain. As *Politico* described his campaign right before he quit:

> It also would complete a spectacular flame-out for the political novice candidate who shot to the top of polls in late September and stayed there for almost two months on the strength of compelling

> debate performances, his outsider appeal and
> catchy '999' tax reform plan.[67]

Catchy, of course, is what rhetoric is all about. Cain created a mesmerizingly simple mantra in his *9-9-9 tax plan*, even if very few people understood its details—indeed, precisely because very few people understood its details. He succeeded in catching people's attention.

But since rhetoric had entirely replaced the substance of his campaign, ultimately he could not withstand the scrutiny that inevitably comes with leading the polls. You can't defend your character from credible attacks by simply refusing to answer questions and repeating "9-9-9," as he actually attempted to do.

Second, repetition cuts against the academic training most people get. I was trained in physics. Most scientists I know do not like to repeat themselves because it implies that they aren't sure of what they are saying. Scientists like to focus on the things that they don't know, since that is the cutting edge of scientific research. They don't keep repeating the things that they do know, which is one reason the public and the media often don't hear from scientists about their strong areas of agreement on global warming.

The climate science deniers, however, are so good at repetition that they continue to repeat myths long after they have been debunked by scientists. Scientists, and the media, grow weary of repeatedly debunking the same lies, the same nonsensical myths. But that, of course, only encourages the deniers to keep repeating those myths. Like my five-year-old daughter, they know that if they just keep repeating the same thing over and over and over and over again, they will eventually get their way.

The Yale Project on Climate Change Communications asked Americans, "If you had the opportunity to talk to an expert on global warming, which of the following questions would you like to ask?"[68] The top question was "How do you know that global warming is caused mostly by human activities, not natural changes in the environment?"

In one sense this is remarkable, since we've known of the central role of human emissions in warming the planet for decades. We call them *greenhouse* gases for a reason. Absent naturally occurring greenhouse gases, the planet would be sixty degrees Fahrenheit colder and inhospitable to life as we know it. But now humans are pouring tens of billions of tons of greenhouse gases into the air each year, primarily by burning coal, oil, and natural gas. And the latest science makes clear that it's "highly likely" all of the warming in the past half century is due to human activities.[69]

But in another sense, it's not remarkable at all that this is the top question. The point is so obvious to most climate scientists that they hardly spend much time talking about it. But the anti-science disinformation campaign has made casting doubt on the "manmade" part of "manmade global warming" a central goal.

If You Don't Repeat, You Can't Compete

They borrowed the tactics from the tobacco industry, which focused relentlessly on casting doubt on the connection between cigarette smoking and cancer, helping to delay restrictions on cigarettes for decades.

Whether for good or ill, repetition works.

To conclude, wowing people requires the repetition of words and phrases, while winning them over requires the repetition of slogans, sentences, and ideas.

CHAPTER FOUR

IRONY: THE TWIST WE CAN'T RESIST FROM SOCRATES TO SEINFELD

No authentic human life is possible without irony.

—Kierkegaard[70]

Irony is a defining feature of the great political orators. Irony is also a defining feature of the great stories through the ages and our own pop culture. If you want true language intelligence, you must master irony in all its forms.

Yet irony remains a hard-to-pin-down concept. A typical dictionary definition is, "The use of words to express something different from and sometimes opposite to their literal meaning." That is verbal irony, a figure of speech.

Because irony is so important to understanding modern American political coverage and popular culture, I'll discuss a few kinds of irony in this chapter. The place to start is with the original irony Socratic irony, the streetwise stratagem for the master orator who wants to win hearts and minds. [71]

1. SOCRATIC IRONY

Irony derives from the Greek *eironeia* ("dissimulation"), the term given to the action and speech of the *eiron*, or "dissembler," a stock character in Greek comedy. The first recorded use is the *Republic* by Plato, where "Socrates himself takes on the role of the eiron" and feigns ignorance as he asks "seemingly innocuous and naïve questions which gradually undermine his inter-locutor's case," trapping him "into seeing the truth." Many Greeks did not see the truth the way Socrates did—they put him to death—so eiron also carries the sense "sly deceiver" or "hypocritical rascal."[72]

Eirons are a stock character in popular culture, most commonly found on police dramas. The top cops on TV routinely play dumb in order to trap the seem-ingly smarter crooks with simple questions that they ask only because they "need to make their report com-plete" or because "the captain is a stickler for details" or they "want to rule you out as a suspect." The greatest of the TV eirons, the one closest to Socrates in spirit, was Peter Falk's Lt. Columbo, one of the most endur-ing TV characters ever created: The pilot aired in 1968, and Peter Falk was still playing the Los Angeles homi-cide detective on special episodes more than thirty-five years later!

Irony: The Twist We Can't Resist

Columbo seems absent-minded and unsophisticated in his rumpled coat. A suspect looking at his disheveled clothes once asked him, "Are you undercover?" to which he replied, "No, underpaid." He is, in fact, much smarter than the polished criminals who think they have committed the perfect crime. His famous catchphrase, "Oh, just one more thing," as he is leaving the room, was invariably followed by an innocuous-sounding question that was key to trapping the crook. When someone says they asked the police commissioner to send "his very best man," Columbo maintains the eiron stance, saying, "My wife says I'm the second-best. She claims there are eighty men tied for first."[73]

On the surface, George W. Bush did not seem eloquent. He also seemed to have a speech impediment that led him to mispronounce or stumble over big words. Interestingly, Churchill suffered from a slight stammer and lisp. Writing of the best orators, Churchill himself pointed out that "sometimes a slight and not unpleasing stammer or impediment has been of some assistance in securing the attention of the audience." It helped Bush.[74]

James Fallows noted before the 2004 presidential debates, "Clearly Bush has been content to let his opponents, including the press, think him a numbskull."[75] If Bush's image was by design, then his oratorical skills were the very definition of irony.[76] Karl Rove called Bush the smartest, best-informed guy in the room. "I've seen it time and time again," Rove told *Newsweek*, "we all get the briefing papers the night before, we've all read them, and he'll inevitably have thought about three steps ahead of anyone in the room." Considering that Rove was called "Bush's Brain," that is either high praise or high irony.[77]

In Shakespeare's *Julius Caesar*, Marc Antony takes on the role of the eiron when he pretends to praise those who killed Caesar even as he whips up the Roman crowd against them. Antony says "I am no orator, as Brutus is, But—as you know me all—a plain blunt man." It is a mark of eirons and wily orators that they accuse their opponents of being rhetoricians. The self-consciously rhetorical Churchill himself once opened an attack on his political opponents saying, "These professional intellectuals who revel in decimals and polysyllables. . . ."[78]

Is it just a coincidence that the only ones who used the word "rhetoric" in the 2004 presidential debates were George Bush and Dick Cheney? In the vice-presidential debate, Cheney said to his Democratic rival, Senator John Edwards, "Your rhetoric, Senator, would be a lot more credible if there was a record to back it up." In the final debate, Bush twice repeated almost verbatim the same accusation about Kerry: "His rhetoric doesn't match his record," and again, "His record in the United States Senate does not match his rhetoric."[79]

Returning to the Roman Forum, we find Marc Antony saying,

Irony: The Twist We Can't Resist

> For I have neither wit, nor words, nor worth,
> Action, nor utterance, nor the power of speech,
> To stir men's blood: I only speak right on; I tell you
> that which you yourselves do know;

So Antony is a man of the people—just reminding them of what they already know. Antony was, in fact, a born patrician, like Bush. Antony was actually a student of rhetoric, but his repeated use of one-syllable words lends an aura of sincerity and credibility to his bluntness. It is a mark of eirons and first-rate orators that they deny eloquence.

Lincoln was a "plain homespun" speaker, or so goes the legend, a legend he himself worked hard to create. In a December 1859 autobiographical sketch provided to a Pennsylvania newspaper, Lincoln explained how his father grew up "literally without education." Lincoln described growing up in "a wild region, with many bears and other wild animals still in the woods. . . . There were some schools, so called." He offers one especially colorful spin: "If a stranger supposed to understand Latin, happened to sojourn in the neighborhood, he was looked upon as a wizzard." No fancy talkers here.

Lincoln explains the result of the little schooling he had: "Of course when I came of age I did not know much." And after that, "I have not been to school since. The little advance I now have upon this store of education, I have picked up from time to time under the pressure of necessity." All this from a man who in the previous year had proven himself to be one of America's greatest intellects and most eloquent orators in the Lincoln-Douglas debates and who during the course of his presidency would demonstrate the most sophisticated grasp of rhetoric of any US president, before or since.[80] Lincoln opened his masterful 1859 Cooper Union speech echoing Antony: "The facts with which I shall deal this evening are mainly old and familiar; nor is there anything new in the general use I shall make of them." (In Antony's own words, "I only speak right on; I tell you that which you yourselves do know.") These are the words of a man who had memorized Shakespeare from William Scott's *Lessons in Elocution*, a treatise that included Antony's famous speech.

The master orator who denies eloquence and rhetoric was such a commonplace by the sixteenth century that Shakespeare resorted to it repeatedly. One reason to study the Bard is that his use of rhetoric has much to tell us about modern politics. "The most common literary allusion to President Bush," wrote columnist Nicholas Kristof in September 2004, "is Shakespeare's Prince Hal, the hard-drinking, wild-living young man who sobers up, reforms and emerges as the great English warrior King Henry V."[81] Hal was also underestimated by his rivals and was a master of oratory, delivering the most famous pre-battle speech in the English language:

Irony: The Twist We Can't Resist

> We few, we happy few, we band of brothers; For
> he today that sheds his blood with me Shall be my
> brother....

Again we see the mark of a great speech: short words
plus repetition. (Bush's 2004 rival was the actual war
hero, a decorated soldier who would try and fail to
make his self-proclaimed "band of brothers" from the
Vietnam War evidence of his fitness to lead the nation.
This is the kind of irony that keeps the figure of speech
fresh after more than two millennia.)

Most interesting, in his very first scene, Hal tells the
audience he plans to "throw off" his loose behavior
because it will make him look more politically attrac-
tive: "My reformation, glittering o'er my fault, Shall
show more goodly and attract more eyes." Thus Hal is
a sly deceiver, a Machiavellian eiron. Two plays later,
after the British triumph at Agincourt, Hal—now King
Henry V—woos Katherine, the daughter of the French
king. Yet, even though Kate's hand was one of Henry's
conditions for peace, the master of rhetoric still treats
us to his tricks.

When Kate says she doesn't speak English well,
Henry says he's glad, "for, if thou couldst, thou wouldst
find me such a plain king that thou wouldst think I had
sold my farm to buy my crown." He's just like a farmer,
a man of the people. He adds, "But, before God, Kate,
I cannot look greenly nor gasp out my eloquence, nor I
have no cunning in protestation; only downright oaths,

which I never use till urged, nor never break for urging."
Like Antony, he disingenuously denies eloquence. The
reason orators use this trick: Being blunt and ineloquent
proves they must perforce be honest and steadfast.

Here is Bush in his Orlando campaign speech on
October 30, 2004:

> Sometimes I'm a little too blunt—I get that from
> my mother. *[Huge cheers]* Sometimes I mangle
> the English language—I get that from my dad.
> *[Laughter and cheers]*
> But you always know where I stand. You can't say
> that for my opponent.[82]

For a blunt language-mangler, that's rousing rhetoric.

Henry urges Kate to "take a fellow of plain and
uncoin'd constancy, for he perforce must do thee
right, because he hath not the gift to woo in other places." Because he is not a clever orator, he must be an
honest and constant man. Then Henry compares himself to an imaginary rival: "For these fellows of infinite
tongue, that can rhyme themselves into ladies' favours,
they do always reason themselves out again." In short,
the other guys are flip-floppers. They talk smarter than I do,
but that's exactly why you can't trust them.

Consider Bush's stump speech in Wilmington,
Ohio, the day before the election, discussing his
September 2003 request for $87 billion in Iraq war
funding and Kerry's vote: "And then he entered the
flip-flop Hall of Fame by saying this: 'I actually did

vote for the $87 billion right before I voted against it.' I haven't spent a lot of time in the coffee shops around here, but I bet you a lot of people don't talk that way." In Burgettstown, two hours later he said, "I doubt many people in western Pennsylvania talk that way." In Sioux City, Iowa, a few hours later, "I haven't spent much time in the coffee shops around here, but I feel pretty comfortable in predicting that not many people talk like that in Sioux land." And in Albuquerque, he said, "I have spent a lot of time in New Mexico, and I've never heard a person talk that way."[83]

Kerry's self-defining and self-defaming quote—"I actually did vote for the $87 billion right before I voted against it"—had the powerful elements of eloquence. Sadly for Kerry, this was the precise reason it sticks in the mind. It had the repetition of two memorable figures found in famous political quotes, *antithesis*, phrases or words put in opposition to each other ("voted for" versus "voted against"), and *chiasmus*, words repeated in inverse order (in this case, "I . . . vote for" and "before I voted"). Little wonder it was ripe for exploitation through sarcasm and repetition.

Why did Kerry flip-flop? Bush had a simple answer. The president told every audience that Kerry's most revealing explanation "was when he said the whole thing was a complicated matter. My fellow Americans, there is nothing complicated about supporting our troops in combat." Rhetoric retains the power to move real people. One attendee at Bush's Orlando rally, Dr.

Richardson-Pinto, was quoted saying: "It doesn't matter if the man [Kerry] can talk. Sometimes, when someone's real articulate, you can't trust what he says, you know?" And Richardson-Pinto is a physician, someone whose credibility depends on being articulate.[84]

The president had everything down cold that we expect from a skilled rhetorician—or at least someone who can follow the script written by a professional logographos: the repeated simple words, the repeated phrases, and the message that his opponent is inconsistent and inconstant because he's too clever by half and doesn't talk the way you and I do. Yet at the same time, Bush manages to leave the impression that he himself is rather slow and inarticulate. In his second term, the disconnect between Bush's rhetoric and his actions would result in a loss of public support, but he managed to get by mostly on rhetoric in 2004.

The flip-flopping charge is not restricted to politics. Those who deny climate science love to use it to attack scientists, who are well known for changing their positions as the evidence changes. The late Michael Crichton offered up the deniers' favorite—but false—charge in his 2004 novel *State of Fear*, when he has one of his fictional environmentalists say, "In the 1970s all the climate scientists believed an ice age was coming." Conservative *Washington Post* columnist George Will has repeated this charge countless times, most recently in September 2011, writing, "In the 1970s, would you have trusted scientists predicting calamity from global cooling?"[85]

Irony: The Twist We Can't Resist

This clever attack tries to make present global-warming fears seem faddish and tries to make climate scientists into flip-floppers. For the record, it just isn't true. A 2008 review of the climate science literature from 1965 to 1979 debunked the "pervasive myth" that scientists were predicting calamity from global cooling or all thought an Ice Age was coming.[86] It concluded that "the possibility of anthropogenic warming dominated the peer-reviewed literature even then." Scientists need to do a better job of explaining how early climate science foreshadowed the climate change we're seeing today, particularly the droughts and extreme weather.

To paraphrase the slogan from the last Democrat to be reelected president, "It's the rhetoric, stupid." And speaking of that famous slogan, it was not merely a vow to focus laser-like on the economy, but a message to the public that Clinton the candidate was definitely not one of those too-smart fellows of infinite tongue, even though, as we all came to learn, he was.

Indeed, Clinton had said in the speech announcing his candidacy for president on October 3, 1991, in Little Rock, Arkansas, "We need more than photo ops and empty rhetoric." In words that would make any eiron proud, he vowed: "This must be a campaign of ideas, not slogans. . . . I'm going to tell you in plain language what I intend to do as president." This was a dig at his opponent, George H. W. Bush, a patrician politician who was not known for his command of the English language but who had not figured out how to turn that to his advantage the way his son later did.

Still, like most successful politicians, Clinton was a master of slogans, including "It's the economy, stupid," "Mend it, don't end it," and "Don't ask, don't tell."

In sum, Socratic irony is the strategy of the master orator who denies eloquence, claiming to be an ordinary Joe, a plain-spoken man of the people.

2. VERBAL IRONY

A second type of irony is best called "verbal irony." The first mention in English is in 1502: "yronye . . . by the whiche a man sayth one & gyveth to understande the contrarye." Verbal irony is a *trope*, from the Greek for *turn*, since it is a figure of speech that turns or changes the meaning of a word away from its literal meaning.[87]

Verbal irony is an essential element of certain kinds of speeches, especially those that occur in a debate or are similarly aimed at disputing a point or rebuking an opponent. Using verbal irony is a powerful means of turning your opponents' arguments against them, by revealing a deeper truth that utterly undercuts their argument. Verbal irony is the way to call your opponent a liar without calling your opponent a "liar."

Often the speaker leaves it up to the audience to find the irony. One rhetoric text used in Elizabethan grammar schools recommends a "Subtle Approach"— winning over the audience "covertly, through dissimulation"—whenever "the hearer has apparently been won over by the previous speakers of the opposition."[88] Such was the case with Marc Antony in *Julius Caesar*. Brutus, in his forum speech, had just convinced the crowd the assassination of Caesar was justified. He convinced them so well that some citizens were persuaded, ironically, that he should be the new Caesar. In making his case, Brutus used the word "honor" four times. Since Brutus was widely respected for his honor, since he directly links the citizens' belief in him to that very honor, Antony needs to attack that quality in him, but do so indirectly, with a "Subtle Approach," since Brutus has won the crowd completely over.

Cleverly, Antony himself uses the word "honorable" ten times in this one speech. He repeatedly says Brutus is an *honourable* man and that all of the conspirators are *honourable*. His irony is increasingly blatant: "When that the poor have cried, Caesar hath wept; Ambition should be made of sterner stuff: Yet Brutus says he was ambitious; And Brutus is an honourable man." With this drumbeat, Antony convinces the crowd that there was no justification for killing Caesar, which in turns means the murder was a *dis*honorable act. For a final knockout punch, Antony reveals the existence of Caesar's will to the citizens, showing them the parchment he describes as the final testament of Caesar's love for them. The citizens beg him to read the will. Antony slyly says:

I have o'ershot myself to tell you of it.
I fear I wrong the honourable men
Whose daggers have stabb'd Caesar; I do fear it.

The crowd is now his. One citizen shouts, "They were traitors," and then spits out, "Honourable men!" This speech is a treatise on verbal irony.

Irony is about having the actual meaning of the words turn out to be the opposite of their literal meaning. Antony uses irony to negate the meaning of "honor" and "honorable" as it applies to Caesar's murderers, using verbal daggers to repeatedly stab Brutus's reputation.

In his crowd-pleasing and career-making Cooper Union speech, Abraham Lincoln used the same rhetorical strategy as Antony—ironic repetition.[89] Much as Antony was not directly debating Brutus, but giving a speech right after him, Lincoln was not directly debating Stephen Douglas, but giving a speech a few months after him. He was offering a very different answer on the crucial "question," as Douglas called it: Is the federal government forbidden from controlling "slavery in our Federal Territories"? Lincoln starts by quoting Douglas for his New York audience:

In his speech last autumn, at Columbus, Ohio, as reported in *The New-York Times*, Senator Douglas said:
"Our fathers, when they framed the Government under which we live, understood this question just as well, and even better, than we do now."

Irony: The Twist We Can't Resist

> I fully indorse this, and I adopt it as a text for this discourse.

"What is the frame of government under which we live?" Lincoln asks rhetorically, as if to clarify Douglas. He immediately helps the audience, "The answer must be: 'The Constitution of the United States.' " He does this so that he can define the "our fathers" in Douglas's speech as the thirty-nine men who signed the Constitution: "I take these 'thirty-nine,' for the present," Lincoln says, "as being 'our fathers who framed the Government under which we live.' "

Then Lincoln begins his brilliant analysis to show that Douglas's words were, in fact, ironic. Douglas had said plainly that the framers of the US government not only understood the slavery issue better than the people in the mid-1800s, but also that they agreed with Douglas. Lincoln grants that the framers understood the slavery issue better but proves that they agreed with him, Abe Lincoln. He examines the voting record of the thirty-nine framers of the Constitution to show that

> . . . twenty-one—a clear majority of the whole—certainly understood that no proper division of local from federal authority, nor any part of the Constitution, forbade the Federal Government to control slavery in the federal territories; while all the rest probably had the same understanding. Such, unquestionably, was the understanding of our fathers who framed the original Constitution;

and the text affirms that they understood the question *better than we.*[90]

Just as Antony threw Brutus's words back in his face, so, too, does Lincoln with Douglas's words. In a masterpiece of ironic repetition comparable to Antony's more famous speech, Lincoln repeats the word "fathers" thirty times, repeats the number "thirty-nine" twenty times, and repeats the entire phrase "Our fathers who framed the Government under which we live" and the phrase "better than we," over twenty times each, presumably with a more sarcastic tone of voice each time (just as a great actor playing Antony would with the word "honorable"), drawing considerable laughter and applause. This is the speech of a man who read Shakespeare often—and aloud.

With a single electrifying speech, masterfully using both Socratic irony and verbal irony, as well as a number of other figures, Honest Abe jump-started a campaign that would win him the Republican nomination and ultimately the presidency. That is language intelligence.

It is a time-tested rhetorical strategy—turning your opponent's words against him, turning them into an ironic commentary on his character or his conclusions. It has become one of the primary political strategies of our own time.

A front-page December 30, 2011, *Washington Post* story, "GOP's election battle plan: Use Obama's own words against him," laid out the Republican battle plan:

> GOP officials in Washington are quietly and methodically finishing what operatives are calling "the book"—500 pages of Obama quotes and video links that will form the backbone of the party's attack strategy against the president leading up to Election Day 2012. . . .

> GOP officials plan to use Obama's words and voice as they build an argument for his defeat: that he made specific promises and entered office with lofty expectations and has failed to deliver on both. . . .

> The new GOP playbook is designed to take one of Obama's great assets—the power of his oratory—and turn it into a liability.[91]

Of course, as the story explains, this is little different from the leaked strategy of the president's team:

> A similar in-his-own-words strategy has already been adopted by Obama's campaign and the Democratic National Committee designed to portray GOP front-runner Mitt Romney as a flip-flopper.

3. DRAMATIC IRONY

One of the central points of irony—of words that mean the opposite of what the speaker says—is that sometimes it is intentional and sometimes not. The first two types of irony I have discussed are intentional. Socrates and Columbo are trying to appear harmless when they are anything but. Antony, with his drumbeat repetition that "Brutus is an honorable man," is being intentionally ironic. By the end of his speech, he is bordering on sarcasm, which "is personal and used with the intention of giving hurt." Sarcasm is the kissing cousin of irony, although since it comes from the Greek for "flesh tearing," perhaps it is better called the biting cousin of irony. [92]

The third type of irony, dramatic irony or situational irony, is the unintentional kind. That is, the person who utters the ironic words or performs the ironic deed is not aware of the irony. The irony is revealed or made obvious by someone else—in a work of fiction, by the author, and in a campaign, by the media or one's political enemies.

Politicians and their speechwriters are on an endless quest for words and images of dramatic irony that can discredit their opponents. They are aided and abetted by journalists trying to find the drama in their personality-driven stories. Think Michael Dukakis in an army tank, or the first President's Bush's unfamiliarity with a grocery store scanner or President George W. Bush on the aircraft carrier with the "Mission Accomplished" banner in the background or the Swift Boat ads run against John Kerry. When John McCain briefly "suspended" his presidential campaign in fall

Irony: The Twist We Can't Resist

2008 because of the financial crisis, the Obama campaign turned an effort by McCain to show leadership into a moment that ironically underscored the "erratic" behavior of their seventy-two-year-old opponent. Understand dramatic irony and you understand both popular culture and politics.

Dramatic irony applies mainly to audiences—such as theatergoers or TV watchers—who know (or are told) the significance of words and actions when the characters do not. Words and pictures that are unintentionally ironic clearly have more force, since they appear to reveal a hidden truth about the speaker—Bush bragging victory in the Iraq war when, as it turns out, the war had hardly begun, or Kerry touting his military record when he could not even defend himself against false verbal attacks by fellow Vietnam veterans. Crafty debaters have always worked hard to turn their opponents' words and deeds against them.

In drama, the audience often knows or quickly learns that the fate awaiting a character is quite different from what the character believes or says. Another character (or the author) may have told us what the truth is or what is going to happen, or we may see it ourselves. For instance, Shakespeare's Iago tells the audience plainly in several early soliloquies that he is a dangerous liar plotting to destroy Othello and the other major characters. So we hear dramatic irony each time one of those characters calls him *honest Iago* or trusts him. We, the audience, know what's going on, but Othello and the others don't.[93]

Modern times are awash in irony. Most sitcoms are ironic, and the most popular, like *Seinfeld* and *The Simpsons*, have tended to be the most ironic. TV shows with narrators who comment on the story are usually drenched in irony, from *Twilight Zone* to *Desperate Housewives*.

Reality shows owe much of their appeal to dramatic irony. The most popular, *American Idol*, begins each season with several shows filled with short episodes of classic dramatic irony: We hear the too-earnest dreams of a young man or woman, how great a singing talent they are, and how this audition will launch them on the road to fame and fortune as the next American Idol. Then we hear them, wailing, shrieking, screaming—anything that can be called making a sound without carrying a tune. And when we take our hands from our ears, and the judges stop laughing, as often as not the contestants are genuinely shocked to be told that they are not going to Hollywood and in fact cannot sing at all. For regular viewers of the show, this is dramatic irony of the purest form, since we know that the contestants' straight-from-the-heart words—their view of reality—is exactly the opposite of what we are about to witness.

These shows are regularly among the most widely watched of the week and indeed of the year. The *American Idol* episode of February 2, 2005, which preceded President Bush's State of the Union Address, drew more viewers on its single network than the address did on the three major networks *combined*! As the *Drudge Report* put it, "The U.S broadcast TV audience would rather watch freaks sing out of tune than President Bush and Democrats wax politics, overnight ratings show."[94] Then again, perhaps we should be reassured that people like to see false idols brought low.

Our greatest movies—whether greatness is defined by either popular acclaim or critical acclaim—define modern irony, literally and figuratively. In *Casablanca*, when Claude Rains shuts down Humphrey Bogart's nightclub, and Bogart asks him, "On what grounds?" he famously replies, "I'm shocked, shocked to find that gambling is going on in here!" just before a croupier hands him a pile of money, saying, "Your winnings, sir." Rains says softly, "Oh, thank you very much," and then loudly, "Everybody out at once!" The "shocked, shocked" line, which is a figure of speech (*epizeuxis*, words repeated one after another for special effect), has itself become a catchphrase for labeling ironic hypocrisy, for telling us when a politician or a person in a position of power is speaking out of both sides of their mouths.

Few events in the twentieth century rival the sinking of the Titanic for irony—try Googling "Titanic" and "irony." So it's no surprise that James Cameron's 1997 movie, *Titanic*, was (until his *Avatar*) the top-grossing movie of all time.[95] Even if the event were not historical, audiences know the dangers of hubris, of early lines such as:

73

"So this is the ship they say is unsinkable."
"It is unsinkable. God himself couldn't sink this ship."[96]

Hubris—arrogant, prideful overconfidence—has an inevitable outcome, as we know from the Bible: "Pride goeth before destruction, and a haughty spirit before a fall." And if the irony is to be complete, the outcome should be self-inflicted:

"So you've not lit the last four boilers then?"
"No, but we're making excellent time."
"Captain, the press knows the size of Titanic, let them marvel at her speed, too. We must give them something new to print. And the maiden voyage of Titanic must make headlines!"

Those final lines are classic dramatic irony, where the speaker has one meaning, but the audience fully understands an entirely other meaning.

The story of the rise and fall of the powerful is as archetypal as formulas gets. It appears in every form of story telling. The story is, for instance, retold in Bob Dylan's classic ballad "Like a Rolling Stone," whose first four words tell us this will be a fable with a traditional moral, "*Once upon a time* you dressed so fine, You threw the bums a dime in your prime, didn't you?" Dylan's heroine starts rich and "proud," but soon she is "without a home" and "scrounging" for her next meal.

What brings irony to these stories is one of two personality-driven plot lines. The first, as we've seen, is hu-

bris or arrogant overconfidence. The second is the no-
tion from psychology that people's greatest strengths
become their greatest weaknesses. In both cases, we have
the fatal wound being self-inflicted, which gives the story
dramatic irony, while we keep a coherent personality for
the protagonist, which gives the story the ring of truth.

These ironic stories touch us not only because we
have read them or watched them so many countless
times in our lives. We have also seen so many instances
in real life, like Richard Nixon or Bill Clinton or Newt
Gingrich, of people brought low by the same traits
that raised them to the heights. And today's report-
ers, like the reporter in *Citizen Kane* trying to figure out
the meaning of Charles Foster Kane's final utterance—
"Rosebud"—are on an endless search for the one word
or symbol that sums up a man's life. President Bush's
father seemed surprised at how a grocery-store scanner
worked, which seemed to connect his patrician past
with the out-of-touch image Clinton was painting of
him. The endless replaying of Howard Dean's screaming exhortation to his supporters following his loss in
the 2004 Iowa caucus became his "Rosebud," an ironically revealing moment of truth. For Dean the passion
that had brought him so far had gone too far.

Dramatic irony, I believe, will become more and
more a core story element for members of the media
who are driven to find dramatic, personality-driven political stories as opposed to hum-drum, policy-driven
ones that focus on issues. There are two key reasons.

First is a clue given to us by the Canadian literary scholar Northrop Frye, that there are four generic plots or storylines: tragedy, comedy, romance, and irony.[97] We see these familiar stories played out every day, day after day, in the news media, in popular culture, and in our own lives, as they have played out in life and literature since the beginning—sometimes in combination, such as romantic-comedies. But political stories are rarely tragedies, seldom comedies, and hardly ever romances. As journalists pursue political drama and storylines that the public has come to expect in both fiction and nonfiction, art and life—as journalists pursue narrative arcs of rise and fall in politics (and perhaps rise again) that have the ring of truth—they are drawn inevitably to the only major plotline left: irony.

Second, the favorite ironic storyline of politics—the self-inflicted wound—is the favorite for a good reason. In this plot line, the victims are not victims of circumstances, and thus deserving of our sympathy rather than repeated humiliation. Nor are they victims of some outside enemy, powerful and evil, and thus deserving of our help rather than our mockery. No, they are victims of their own flaws and excesses. They deserved what they got—and the media does well to point them out, as a lesson to us all.

And this brings us to the last of the four kinds of irony, irony of fate.

4. IRONY OF FATE: POETIC JUSTICE

The irony underlying poetic justice occurs when a character, or a real person, gets the fate that they deserve, typically the very opposite of the one that they themselves expect or plan for. It is embodied in the concept of karma, in the popular phrase "what goes around comes around." It is a comeuppance. Poetic justice is essentially the figure of speech turned into a dramatic device, for as one Elizabethan writer explains, the use of verbal irony is "chiefly to reprove by derision."[98]

Poetic justice is "a rational distribution of rewards and punishments that represented the cosmos as designed and controlled by a benign Providence," writes John Andrews, the former director of the Folger Shakespeare Library. So, almost by definition, poetic justice is a core motif in the Bible. When people lie to God or disobey Him or break His commandments, judgment is meted out "by a benign Providence." We see this in all of the great stories, starting with Adam and Eve, and Cain and Abel, through to the very end of the Bible.[99]

The enduring popularity of the biblical version of poetic justice found in Revelation is seen in the enormous popularity of the *Left Behind* series, with over 65 million books sold in a series that fictionalizes the Rapture and the end of days. Here God metes out his harshest, hellish punishment upon the sinners and non-believers, and His greatest rewards to the faithful.

Poetic justice of all kinds is extremely common in popular culture. At the most basic level, in the vast majority of TV shows, movies, plays, and books, good triumphs over evil. Good is rewarded, evil is destroyed, criminals are captured, boy gets girl. This is so commonplace now that it hardly seems ironic, unless a special twist is added, which the best writers have always done. Indeed, the most ironic form of poetic justice is best told in a song by two masters of irony, Gilbert and Sullivan, in their classic comic opera, *Mikado.* In the musical, the Mikado, the powerful and pompous ruler of Japan, describes his vision of poetic justice:

> My object all sublime I shall achieve in time—
> To let the punishment fit the crime, The punishment fit the crime;
>
> And make each pris'ner pent, Unwillingly represent
>
> A source of innocent merriment, Of innocent merriment!

This is the chorus, which is repeated another five times. In the verses, they give us examples of their brand of poetic justice. For instance, society's dull speakers will be forced to "hear sermons from mystical Germans who preach from ten till four" (which is reason enough to study rhetoric).

The repeated phrase "innocent merriment" from the chorus is grounded in a profound insight. We enjoy seeing people get what they deserve in the most fitting fashion. In our unfair world, we yearn to see justice, and the more poetic the better.

As Hamlet put it, "'tis sport to have the enginer" [the "maker of engines of war"] "hoist with his own petard" ["blown into the air by his own bomb"]. The non-lethal version of this kind of poetic justice—farcical schemes of sitcom stars blowing up in their faces—has been a staple of classic comedies, like *The Honeymooners* and *I Love Lucy*, and modern ones, like *The Simpsons*. This source of innocent merriment was perfected in that most successful of modern sitcoms, *Seinfeld*, which *TV Guide* named the greatest TV show of all time.[100]

Missing the point, critics often described *Seinfeld* as a "show about nothing." Some cultural critics even denounced the show for glamorizing a kind of ironic detachment, when the reverse was true.[101] In the vast majority of episodes, the plot was contrived to ensure that whatever deceit or trickery or hubristic cleverness is employed by the main characters at the start comes back to bite them at the end.

Jerry believes, to take one episode, that the breasts of a beautiful woman he has started to date, Sidra (Teri Hatcher), must be fake. To uncover the truth he enlists his friend Elaine, who learns they are, in fact, real when she trips in a sauna and grabs them. The audience knows this plot must inevitably backfire. And it does. Jerry, upon learning the breasts are real, invites Sidra to his apartment, but just seconds before Jerry is going to see the breasts, Sidra sees Elaine and walks out on Jerry, saying, "And by the way, they're real, and they're spectacular." Jerry is not rewarded for his shallowness. He is punished for it, and Elaine says to him, "Just when I think you're the shallowest man I've ever met, you somehow manage to drain a little more out of the pool."[102] The breasts were real, but Jerry was not. He was deceitful. That is irony of fate.

The show's finale in 1998 was the ultimate karmic backlash. Many of the people whom Jerry and his friends had harmed over the years through their selfish and deceitful behavior, including Sidra, return to testify against them. Their "crimes" exposed, they end the show in jail, thus receiving both literal and figurative poetic justice. That's innocent merriment.

Shakespeare metes out harsh poetic justice to most every major character. Brutus decides to murder Caesar because he fears that if Caesar is crowned king, he may become a tyrant. "He would be crown'd: How that might change his nature, there's the question." So the greatest poetic justice that Shakespeare can deliver is to have Brutus's nature changed after he kills Caesar and acquires some of Caesar's power. Shakespeare makes clear in the play's second half that Brutus has become like Caesar himself, arrogant and egotistical. Brutus becomes like the person he helped murder, and, soon after, kills himself with the same sword he used to stab Caesar, hoist with his own petard.

That people who acquire power become what they once opposed is another standard ironic plotline, from

Irony: The Twist We Can't Resist

Orson Welles' *Citizen Kane* and George Orwell's *Animal Farm* to *All the King's Men*. In the first three episodes of the Star Wars saga, good Jedi hero Anakin Skywalker transforms into evil Jedi-slayer Darth Vader, the dark father. In ironic dramas, power always corrupts. To the extent that the media is increasingly treating politics as an ironic drama, the story line of corrupting power will inevitably become more commonplace. This is especially true since the story line has so much human truth in it. In June 2004, when Bill Clinton was asked by Dan Rather on *60 Minutes* why he had had an affair with Monica Lewinsky, he replied, "I think I did something for the worst possible reason—just because I could."[103]

In life as in drama, power does, in fact, corrupt.

The other iconic ironic storyline is the reverse of power transforming good to evil: Love transforms evil to good. This is standard fare in comedies, like *Pretty Woman*, where the love of Julia Roberts, the prostitute with a heart of gold (an archetype that itself has become a cliché) transforms Richard Gere from a hard-hearted, job-destroying corporate raider into a soft-hearted job-rescuing corporation saver. And in episodes Four, Five, and Six of *Star Wars*, we see the transformation of Darth Vader, ally to the evil emperor, back to good Anakin Skywalker, destroyer of the emperor, because of the love of his son, Luke Skywalker. This story line also has power because it has truth. People are transformed every day by love, the love of a good man or woman, of family, of God.

At the heart of American culture and politics is irony, irony in all of its forms—Socratic, verbal, dramatic, and poetic justice. The most successful modern politicians are plain-spoken eirons: Clinton and Bush. The most successful TV shows are the most overtly ironic.

We live in a time when the "news" show with the hottest buzz is a fake news show, *The Daily Show*, perhaps the most overtly ironic show in TV history. But that may just be an inevitable outcome of today's super-cynical politics. As host Jon Stewart once said of the Bush Administration, "I really think their foreign-policy goal is to spread irony throughout the world."[104]

Irony in all of its forms *works*, both in art and in life, so we will never stop seeing and hearing more of it. Let's look at the forefather of irony and repetition.

CHAPTER FIVE

WHAT EVIL LURKS IN THE HEARTS OF MEN? THE FORESHADOW KNOWS

Give me the child until he is seven, and I will show you the man.

—Jesuit maxim

As a theatrical device, the essence of foreshadowing can be found in Anton Chekhov's advice to a novice playwright: "If there is a gun hanging on the wall in the first act, it must fire in the last."[105] Create anticipation and then fulfill the listener's desire.

Foreshadowing is the flip side or, more accurately, the prequel of repetition—and of irony, as well, for if a person's words or deeds are to become ironic, they must be foreshadowed, they must be hinted at early on. When a scheme is hatched in the first act of a Shakespeare play or the opening minutes of a sitcom, it must—*must*—backfire in the end.

Foreshadowing is related to the figure of speech *ominatio* (Latin for "omen"). In *Julius Caesar*, Shakespeare has a soothsayer famously and futilely warn Caesar, "Beware the Ides of March"—a foreshadowing ominatio that Caesar famously and fatally ignores: "He is a dreamer," shrugs Caesar. "Let us leave him."

Bob Dylan's tragic "Like a Rolling Stone" heroine is similarly warned, and by many: "Beware, doll, you're bound to fall"—which she also unwisely pays no heed to: "You thought they were all kiddin' you."

Dramatic foreshadowing has an even more important rhetorical counterpart. The golden rule of speechmaking is "*Tell 'em what what you're going to tell 'em; tell 'em; then tell 'em what you told 'em.*" The first part of that triptych is the rhetorical foreshadowing of the main idea of your speech, the introduction of the dominant theme of your remarks.

I HAVE A DREAM

I can think of no more remarkable combination of dramatic and rhetorical foreshadowing in a modern public address than the opening lines of Martin Luther King's keynote address at the August 1963 March on Washington for Jobs and Freedom, delivered on the steps of the Lincoln Memorial. The speech is often presented without his introductory sentence, which is unfortunate since it is an essential element of his message.

King began, "I am happy to join with you today in what will go down in *history* as the greatest demonstration for freedom in the *history* of our nation."

The Foreshadow Knows

This opening line foreshadows that the intellectual focus of the speech will be "freedom," a word that, with its partner "free," King repeats twenty-four times in his fifteen-hundred-word oration. As we will soon see, it also anticipates his optimistic message.

King uses the word "history" twice in this simple prefatory line, foreshadowing that he will be taking a historical perspective, which he does from the start.

> Five score years ago, a great American, in whose symbolic shadow we stand, signed the Emancipation Proclamation. This momentous decree came as a great beacon light of hope to millions of Negro slaves who had been seared in the flames of withering injustice. It came as a joyous daybreak to end the long night of captivity.

Echoing Lincoln's famous formulation, "fourscore and seven years ago," in the literal shadow of the Lincoln monument, King here combines the verbal with the visual to turn Lincoln's two great 1863 acts of communication—the Emancipation Proclamation and Gettysburg Address—into a symbolic foreshadowing of his own remarks one hundred years later. In doubling this historical connection, he underscores what will be his main theme: Emancipation has not yet been realized:

> But one hundred years later, we must face the tragic fact that the Negro is still not free. One hundred years later, the life of the Negro is still sadly crippled by the manacles of segregation and the chains of discrimination. One hundred years later,

the Negro lives on a lonely island of poverty in the midst of a vast ocean of material prosperity. One hundred years later, the Negro is still languishing in the corners of American society and finds himself an exile in his own land. So we have come here today to dramatize an appalling condition.

We hear again King's favorite rhetorical device in this speech, anaphora, in the repetition of "one hundred years later" to help him refine the central idea that "the Negro is still not free." King's speech makes the words "Emancipation Proclamation" cruelly ironic: The Negro was proclaimed free, but still is not.

The body of the speech lays out King's nonviolent approach to fulfilling the "quest for freedom" and restates again and again both his dream and his demand for freedom. He says that "in spite of the difficulties and frustrations of the moment, I still have a dream . . . a dream deeply rooted in the American dream." An essential goal of the speech is to instill hope, optimism, and faith in the listeners that the dream of freedom will be achieved, to urge with a powerful metaphor that they "not seek to satisfy our thirst for freedom by drinking from the cup of bitterness and hatred." He describes his stirring dreams, which are themselves ominatio, foretelling a future without racism, a future of freedom for all. He builds to the climax using the phrase "Let freedom ring" a dozen times and ends with the final repetitions of the key word as he says we can "speed up that day when all of God's children . . . will be able to join hands and sing in the words of the old Negro spiritual, 'Free at last! Free at last! Thank God Almighty, we are free at last!'"

Now we see what was foreshadowed in the opening line: "I am happy to join with you today in what will go down in history as the greatest demonstration for freedom in the history of our nation." He is foreshadowing—prophesying—the success of this demonstration and the realization of his dreams.

That King would be a master of rhetoric and foreshadowing is not unexpected since he was, after all, a reverend, a preacher, a student of the Bible. Foreshadowing and ominatio are the foundation upon which the Bible's scaffolding of rhetoric was built—and the power of dreams to foretell the future is a biblical truism. For Christians, the words in the Old Testament foreshadow the coming of the Messiah in the New Testament. The gospels are clearly written to echo the prophecies and promises and proverbs in the Old Testament. If you are a believer, that is because Jesus *is* the Messiah, the fulfillment of the words in the Old Testament. If you are not a believer, that is because the writers of the New Testament were trying to portray Jesus as the Messiah. Either way, by God's design or man's, the Old Testament foreshadows the New Testament again and again.

Jesus himself makes many prophecies. He foretells events that happen very soon, such as when he tells Peter, "Verily I say unto thee, That this night, before the cock crow, thou shalt deny me thrice." He foretells events a long time off: "And I say also unto thee, That thou art Peter, and upon this rock I will build my church; and the gates of hell shall not prevail against it." And he foretells events that have not yet come to pass—his return.

Foreshadowing and ominatio are key elements of poetic justice. Consider the story of Joseph. His brothers hated him because their father loved him the most, which the gift of the coat of many colors showed only too clearly. Joseph dreamt that he and his brothers were collecting stalks of grain, and when his own grain stalk stood up, those of his brothers bowed down before him. "Shalt thou indeed reign over us?" his brothers said. The text goes on, "And they hated him yet the more for his dreams, and for his words." Dreams are classic foreshadowing in the Bible as well as many other holy books.[106]

One day, when Joseph's brothers saw him in the field, "they said one to another, 'Behold, this dreamer cometh. Come now therefore, and let us slay him, and cast him into some pit . . . *and we shall see what will become of his dreams.*'" This is best labeled ironic foreshadowing, a favorite device also of Shakespeare's and other great writers. The final line is intended as sarcasm, that the dreams will be dashed in death, but it soon becomes dramatic irony.

Instead of killing him, his brothers sold him into slavery. Joseph ended up in the Egyptian prison, but using his power to interpret dreams, he not only won his freedom but soon became Pharaoh's right-hand man, after predicting that Pharaoh's dream of seven lean cows eating seven fat cows meant there would be seven good harvests followed by seven years of famine, and thus, during the good years, Pharaoh would need to store up the grain. Every single thing Joseph said comes true. Then, during the famine, Jacob sent his sons to Egypt for grain so the family would not starve. Joseph thus gained power over his brothers, whom he put through various trials. But instead of seeking revenge, he saved his family from starvation.

This is poetic justice: Joseph's dreams of having power over his brothers came true precisely because they had abandoned him, making their words dramatic irony that foreshadowed the end of the story. This is irony of fate.

The enduring power and poignancy of this story can be found in the words on a plaque at the Lorraine Motel, in Memphis, Tennessee, the site of Martin Luther King's assassination (with a slightly different translation than the King James): "*Behold the dreamer. Let us slay him, and we will see what will become of his dream.*"

FORESHADOWING AND SHAKESPEARE

The master of ironic foreshadowing leading to poetic justice is Shakespeare. The Bard of Avon metes out harsh poetic justice to every major character in his tragedies. Every single ironic fate is foreshadowed. Iago spends most of *Othello* as a master puppeteer using his rhetorical powers to pull the strings of the main characters, convincing Othello to murder his faithful wife, Desdemona. But in the play's final scene, Iago himself becomes a wife-murderer. Shakespeare had foreshadowed this ironic ending in an early soliloquy, when Iago says he suspects his wife has committed adultery with Othello and suggests his own actions are driven by a desire for revenge. Iago vows, "And nothing can or shall content my soul *Till I am even'd with him, wife for wife.*" How prophetic. He does become evened with the Moor, wife for wife, with the final ironic twist that the Moor's wife dies lying to protect her husband, while Iago's wife dies telling the truth to destroy her husband.

Because his wife speaks out, Iago's evil is revealed to all, which brings him the most horrible fate of all, prolonged torture: "For this slave, if there be any cunning cruelty that can *torment* him much and hold him long" ["keep him alive a long time before he dies"], "It shall be his." Shakespeare foreshadows this in the third scene, when, after learning Desdemona is lost to him (because Othello's marriage to her will not be reversed), Roderigo says he will commit suicide: "It is silliness to live when to live is *torment.*" This line can now be seen to be a brilliantly ironic judgment in advance by Roderigo (and Shakespeare). Though he may be a relatively simple-minded man whom Iago disdains and ultimately kills, Roderigo is smart enough to know that death is far better than prolonged torture.

WHY FORESHADOWING IS HERE TO STAY

Foreshadowing works for two reasons. First, as described here and in the last chapter, the great stories, from the Greek myths and the Bible to Shakespeare and popular culture, are constructed around irony, around poetic justice that is foreshadowed or forewarned. In *Citizen Kane*, Orson Welles brilliantly starts with Kane's dying word, "Rosebud," and ends with the audience learning that Rosebud is the name of Kane's childhood sled and thus represents his lost innocence and the only time he was really happy. This leads to the second reason we are enthralled by foreshadowing.

Ultimately, the reason foreshadowing works, and the reason we can expect more of it in popular culture and political coverage is that we like to believe that people's individual lives have a circularity, a consistency—a pattern. We see that repetition ourselves—the people around us making the same decisions, the same mistakes, over and over again, and, if we achieve some wisdom and self-awareness in our own lives, we realize we repeat ourselves, too. As one example, in *Getting the Love You Want*, one of the basic texts for couples' therapists, Harville Hendrix explains that one of the most reliable indicators for why someone falls in love with you is that your negative qualities match those of their opposite sex parent or caregiver. Thus do we tend to relive the same story as our parents.

Consider an example well-known to social scientists—the "Linda-the-bank-teller problem."[107] Two researchers gave students the following description of a hypothetical person:

> Linda is 31 years old, single, outspoken, and very bright. She majored in philosophy. As a student, she was deeply concerned with issues of discrimination and social justice, and also participated in anti-nuclear demonstrations.

They then had the students rank several statements about Linda on a 1-to-8 scale with 1 being the least probable and 8 being the most probable. Two of the eight statements were as follows:

- Linda is a bank teller. (*T*)
- Linda is a bank teller and is active in the feminist movement. (*T&F*)

From a purely logical or statistical perspective, statement *T* must be more probable than statement *T&F*, since the latter statement presupposes the former is true. And yet when either graduate and medical students with statistical training or PhD candidates in Stanford Business School's Decision Science Program were given this question, more than four-fifths in each group ranked *T&F* as more probable than *T*. They thought it was more likely that Linda was a bank teller *and* a feminist than just a bank teller alone. This result caused a big stir among social scientists, but should not be so surprising. We think in terms of a whole person, and we try to scratch out a consistent story from whatever facts we get. The original description doesn't match Linda-the-bank-teller that well, but makes more sense for Linda-the-feminist-bank-teller. Our thinking processes are not purely logical, especially when we are judging other people. As one student remarked after the statistical mistake was pointed out, "I thought you only asked for my opinion."

The Jesuits have a maxim, "Give me the child until he is seven, and I will show you the man." Director Michael Apted built an entire series of films around this idea, that the child foreshadows the man (or woman). He started with *Seven Up*, the 1964 film that began to track the lives of fourteen British youngsters, followed by movies that revisit them every seven years, the most recent being *49 Up* (2006). The films show that even seven-year-olds can demonstrate a prophetic view of how their lives will unfold, and that there is indeed much of the child in the adult, and vice versa.

Politicians and the media believe that the public believes in foreshadowing. Why else do so many politicians spend so much time telling their personal life story? Why do so many political eirons spend so much time crafting a story of humble beginnings? Why do so many journalists spend so much time retelling the politicians' stories? Why do so many journalists spend so much time digging up specks of dirt from the distant past, looking for an event or a symbol that casts a shadow over—or perhaps eclipses entirely—a politicians' entire career?

Why else would a prominent US politician, Senator Joseph Biden, pursuing the Democratic presidential nomination in 1987, plagiarize his life story from a British politician, Neil Kinnock?[108]

Kinnock (original)	Biden
Why am I the first Kinnock in a thousand generations to be able to get to university? Why is Glenys the first woman in her family in a thousand generations to be able to get to university?	I started thinking as I was coming over here, why is it that Joe Biden is the first in his family ever to go to a university? Why is it that my wife, who is sitting out there in the audience, is the first in her family to ever go to college?
Was it because all our predecessors were thick? . . . Does anybody really think that they didn't get what we had because they didn't have the talent or the strength or the endurance or the commitment? Of course not. It was because there was no platform upon which they could stand.	Is it because our fathers and mothers were not bright? . . . No, it's not because they weren't as smart. It's not because they didn't work as hard. It's because they didn't have a platform upon which to stand.

The Foreshadow Knows

You can feel the power of the words, the repetitions, the rhetorical questions, as the classic story of humble beginnings is connected directly to the politician's passion for helping the less privileged. What else accounts for the plagiarism if not the pressure to deliver compelling oratory on one's origins in a time when most US politicians lack the language intelligence to compose their own memorable lines? The supreme irony is that when the plagiarism was uncovered, the phony foreshadowing overshadowed everything else Biden had done and became yet another example of how dramatic irony undermined a politician, how a candidate was hoist with his petard.

And since the media is increasingly focused on personalities and entertainment, on storytelling and drama, the pressure to find (or invent) foreshadowing will grow only more intense. Why else do so many otherwise smart politicians exaggerate their military service or otherwise inflate their resume?

The media bards want an epic song to sing, and the best politicians want to write the lyrics. At a Social Security rally with her son in March 2005, Barbara Bush shared with the audience the story of a stubborn child, concluding, "So, now you can see where the president's tenaciousness comes from—which people also seem to admire so much. It's what you want in a president; it's not what you want in a six-year-old."[109] Give me the child until he is six, and I will show you the president.

Joseph J Romm

The 2004 presidential campaign revealed how foreshadowing had moved to the forefront of modern political campaigns. With huge issues facing the country—terrorism, the war in Iraq, Social Security, healthcare—the candidates and their allies and the media were obsessed throughout with finding fateful foreshadowing. John Kerry based much of his primary campaign, nominating convention, and presidential campaign on events that had taken place more than thirty years earlier in Vietnam. He tried to show that his heroic military deeds as a young man both revealed his character as a man and foretold that he would be heroic again, this time in the war on terror—making him a sound choice to be commander-in-chief.

Kerry, however, made two fatal mistakes in his foreshadowing effort that we can learn from. First, he never linked the second half of his life to the first half, never completed the life story, to show that the foreshadowing had in fact foreshadowed anything. Second, if you are going to build a campaign around some foreshadowing event, you must defend your story against the inevitable attacks. Your opponents understand the power of foreshadowing and will not just sit by while you write the story you want. In Kerry's case, the political group Swift Boat Veterans for Truth launched a frontal assault on his foreshadowing. They accused Kerry of making up or exaggerating almost every fact, and Kerry did not fight back, which undermined his message of being a fighter both directly and symbolically—even though virtually every claim by the ironically named group turned out to be false. The key point here is that if you don't create *and defend* a complete and plausible extended metaphor for your campaign, you cannot win.

In Bush's case, too, the media and his opponents pursued his youthful indiscretions like the relentless Inspector Javert in *Les Miserables*, or, to use a more modern simile, like the Terminator. In the 2000 campaign, Bush famously used a first-class piece of rhetorical repetition as a universal defense against all journalist questions aimed at finding the fateful foreshadowing, such as cocaine use: "When I was young and irresponsible, I was young and irresponsible."

This is why so many in the Tea Party movement have spent so much time questioning Obama's birth in Hawaii and his religion—to find the foreshadowing for their phony argument that Obama is "not one of us," not American and not a true Christian.

To sum up, foreshadowing works in life for the same reason it works in art: People like straightforward stories and coherent characters. They like a beginning, middle, and end that somehow connect. If the Golden Rule of speechmaking is "Tell 'em what you're going to tell 'em; then tell 'em; then tell 'em what you told 'em," then the Golden Rule of political storytelling is, "Tell them where you came from, then tell them who you are, then tell them what you're going to do"—but make certain that it's all part of the same story (and the same extended metaphor).

CHAPTER SIX

METAPHORICAL MISSILES AND MINEFIELDS

The greatest thing by far is to be a master of metaphor.

—Aristotle

Metaphors are the Lexus of figures. Or, to put it more aptly, metaphors are the Toyota Prius of figures because a metaphor is a hybrid, connecting two dissimilar things to achieve a unique turn of phrase.

Metaphors are bolder than their younger siblings, similes. If I tell my sweetheart in a simile, "You are *as* sweet *as* honey," or "You are sweet *like* honey," that is sweet of me, but how much sharper she will hear, "You are honey." Similes are more true in *fact*, whereas metaphors are more true in *feeling*.[110] Similes play it safe, like a trapeze artist with a net, whereas metaphors soar through the air with no thought of the risk.

Yet metaphors are always risky because they are not hedged. I am saying you don't just resemble honey (in only one respect—sweetness), you are honey itself

99

in every respect. I leave so much to the imagination or to your own bad experience: Your sweetheart's father might be a beekeeper, and she might think of honey as something that gets her stung repeatedly. Metaphors are much more prone to misuse and misinterpretation than other figures, as we'll see.

"To be a master of metaphor," Aristotle writes in *Poetics*, is "a sign of genius, since a good metaphor implies *intuitive perception of the similarity in dissimilars.*"

WHY METAPHORS MOVE US

Social science research has put metaphors atop Mount Olympus. The journal *Cognitive Science* explains:

> Extensive studies and analyses have been done on a broad range of our most basic concepts, such as time, cause, event, mind, thought, memory, self, knowledge, morality, etc. These studies reveal that *virtually all of our abstract conceptualization and reasoning is structured by metaphor.*[111]

Metaphors are not just a pleasing figure of speech we use by chance. They reflect the very structure of our thinking and of our brain itself. Edward O. Wilson argued in his book *Biophilia*, "The brain depends upon elegance to compensate for its own small size and short lifetime." As we evolved, the brain "was forced to rely on tricks to enlarge memory and speed computation." Hence, the human mind "specializes on analogy and metaphor, on a sweeping together of chaotic sensory experience into workable categories labeled by words and stacked into hierarchies for quick recovery."[112]

University of Arizona students were asked one of two questions: "How many murders were there last year in Detroit?" or "How many murders were there last year in Michigan?"[113] The median answer the students gave for city of Detroit was two hundred murders and, for the whole state of Michigan, one hundred. In fact, the rest of Michigan has almost as many murders every year as its most deadly city. But "Detroit" is a much more dangerous-*sounding* place than "Michigan." Detroit has become a metaphor for violence and urban decay, and that metaphor frames the answer students give. I will explore how metaphors frame our thinking in the next chapter.

Metaphors are easier to remember than literal statements with the same meaning. This is true even of archaic metaphors from Shakespeare. Lines such as "Your bait of falsehood takes this carp of truth" (by Polonius in *Hamlet*) were better recognized on a later memory test than lines with the same meaning but modern phrasing, such as "Your offering of falsehood takes this gift of truth."[114]

Metaphors make it easier to understand and remember prose. People were asked to read short passages on a subject such as how Hitler "committed his people to a course of war." The passages either ended with a literal summary line, "The German people blindly accepted Hitler's dangerous ideas," or a metaphorical one, "The sheep followed the leader over the cliff." Then everyone was tested for how well they recalled the material. You might expect that the picture was sticky— but the metaphor was more like a weld: "Not only were the concluding metaphors themselves better remembered than the literal paraphrases, but there was also an increase in recall of the preceding context."[115]

Metaphors enhance our memories in at least two ways. First, they create another place in the brain for a word or phrase to reside. People remember words better when they have multiple ways to remember them, such as combining repetition and a rhyme ("Double your pleasure, double your fun with Doublemint Doublemint Doublemint gum!"). In particular, metaphors create a visual aid to memory. Metaphor is "used for the sake of creating a vivid mental picture," wrote the author of one of the rhetoric textbooks used to teach Elizabethan children.[116] Take a look at the pictures painted by a small menagerie of Shakespeare's most memorable metaphors:

All the world's a stage	*the dogs of war*
jealousy as the *green-eyed monster*	*in my mind's eye,*
to *wear my heart upon my sleeve*	*a tower of strength*
the milk of human kindness	*vaulting ambition*
There is a tide in the affairs of men	*the world's mine oyster*
who steals my purse steals trash	music as the *food of love*

Good talkers far outnumber great speechmakers in part because good talkers tend to be highly verbal people with a strong ability to make remarks that are pleasing to the ear. They are not necessarily so talented at persuading those who learn better with their other senses. Language intelligence means being able to persuade all types, not just the highly verbal, but also, for instance, the highly visual, who make up a large portion of our population. Metaphors are one of the best ways to verbally connect to visual people, and those with high language intelligence are good at painting pictures with words—the *green-eyed monster* that is jealousy.

Metaphors aid in memory a second way: They require the hearer or reader to *think* more, to light up more brain circuits, to figure out the connections and what they mean. As one study of "Figures of Rhetoric in Advertising Language" put it (in muddy jargon that no ad writer would use), "Effortfully processed information is more readily retrieved from memory than less effortfully processed information."[117] That is, the more involved you are in decoding a message, the more it sticks (Budweiser is "the King of Beers," Chevy trucks are "Like a Rock").

Ideally, a metaphor will make you think *and* at the same time create a visual image that connects to something already residing in your memory, such as the image of sheep being herded and blindly following a shepherd.

THE WEAPONS OF POLITICAL WAR

Given their power, metaphors have naturally become a weapon wielded by all great political speechmakers.

Lincoln, a devout student of the two great rhetoric texts, the Bible and Shakespeare, understood that power more than any other president. In 1848, when he was a Whig in Congress, he responded to the claim that his party had "taken shelter under General Taylor's military coat-tail," referring to Zachary Taylor, the Whig Party presidential nominee. He turned the metaphor against his opponents, saying they themselves had run under the coat-tail of General Jackson for five elections. Then, instructing them in rhetoric, Lincoln added "military coat-tails, or tails of any sort, are not figures of speech such as I would be the first to introduce into discussions here."[118]

Lincoln launched a metaphor of his own, wishing the "gentlemen on the other side to understand that the use of degrading figures is a game at which they may not find themselves able to take all the winnings." At this point, some in the opposition cried, "We give it up!" But Lincoln was just warming up. His reply was a rhetorical cruise missile:

> Aye, you give it up, and well you may; but for a very different reason from that which you would have us understand. *The point—the power to hurt—of all figures consists in the truthfulness of their application*; and, understanding this, you may well give it up. They are weapons which hit you, but miss us.

The opposition was hoist with their own metaphorical petard.

Lincoln offered his most poignant metaphor in a June 1858 speech to the Illinois Republican state convention after they had chosen him as their candidate to run against Democrat Stephen Douglas in the US Senate race: "A house divided against itself cannot stand." He then amplified the metaphor by listing divisions, one after another:

> I believe this government cannot endure, permanently half *slave* and half *free*. I do not expect the Union to be *dissolved*—I do not expect the house to *fall*—but I do expect it will cease to be *divided*. It will become all *one thing* or all *the other*.
>
> Either the *opponents* of slavery, will arrest the further spread of it, and place it where the public mind shall rest in the belief that it is in the course of ultimate extinction; or its *advocates* will push it forward, till it shall become alike lawful in all the States, *old* as well as *new*—*North* as well as *South*.

We learn from Lincoln's partner in law, William Herndon, that Lincoln wanted to use "some universally known figure [of speech] expressed in simple language . . . that may strike home to the minds of men in order to raise them up to the peril of the times." The power of the metaphor of the Union as a house is not merely its visual simplicity, but in the link to the gospels. Lincoln is quoting Jesus, implying that God is on the side of those who think like he does, that slavery must die and soon. Lincoln lost the Senate race, and some thought that he had lost because of this speech,

Joseph J Romm

because his message was too strong. But if the metaphor cost him the Senate, Lincoln's brilliant extension
of the metaphor in the speech would cost Douglas the
presidency, as we will see in the next chapter.

Winston Churchill had a keen sense of the unique
power of metaphors even at the age of twenty-two:

> [T]he influence exercised over the human mind
> by apt analogies is and has always been immense.
> Whether they translate an established truth into
> simple language or whether they adventurously
> aspire to reveal the unknown, they are among
> the most formidable weapons of the rhetorician.
> The effect upon the most cultivated audiences is
> electrical.... One such will make a speech or mar
> a measure.[119]

Churchill used a great many metaphors, some blunt—
"dictators ride to and fro upon tigers which they dare
not dismount. And the tigers are getting hungry"—and
some more poetic: "History with its flickering lamp
stumbles along the trail of the past, trying to recon-
struct its scenes, to revive its echoes, and kindle with
the pale gleams the passion of the former days." At sev-
enty-one, he gave us his most memorable metaphor, in
a March 1946 speech in Fulton, Missouri, that displays
his signature "rhymeless, meterless verse":

> A shadow has fallen upon the scene
> so lately lighted by the Allied victory....
> From Stettin in the Baltic

to Trieste in the Adriatic,
an *iron curtain* has descended across the Continent.

A single, well-crafted metaphor, like a well-crafted building, can endure for ages.

A 2005 study on "Presidential Leadership and Charisma" examined the use of metaphors in the first-term inaugural addresses of three dozen presidents who had been independently rated for charisma. The conclusion: "Charismatic presidents used nearly twice as many metaphors (adjusted for speech length) than non-charismatic presidents." Additionally, when students were asked to read a random group of inaugural addresses and highlight the passages they viewed as most inspiring, "even those presidents who did not appear to be charismatic were still perceived to be more inspiring when they used metaphors."[120]

Obama is not a metaphorical man. Contrast Clinton's metaphorical "bridge to the 21st century" with Obama's effort to launch a comparable slogan of his own, "winning the future." The literal phrase conjures no image and was universally panned. I can't find a single person in the messaging business who thinks it works. Even Obama only halfheartedly repeats it from time to time in major speeches.

Scientists have generally not been metaphorical either. Scientific training, at least as I experienced it, emphasizes sticking to facts and speaking literally. Scientific debates are won by those whose theory best explains the facts, not by the most gifted speakers. This view of science is perhaps best summed up in the motto of the Royal Society of London, one of the world's oldest scientific academies (founded in 1660), *Nullius in verba*: Take nobody's word. Words alone are not science.

Many climate scientists are beginning to realize that they have not been winning the communications war with the disinformation campaigners and that metaphors can be a powerful tool for explaining complicated scientific ideas. For instance, how can one convey the fact that human emissions have a powerful warming effect on the earth? One Australian scientist explained that the warming from carbon dioxide we've already put in the air equals one million Hiroshima bombs detonated every day. Suddenly, the abstract concept becomes real and potent.

What is a good way to explain the science that says global warming is making record-smashing extreme weather events more frequent and more destructive, but is not actually "causing" the entire disaster? Meteorologist Dr. Jeff Masters did a great job on the *PBS News Hour* in December 2011: "We look at heat waves, droughts, and flooding events. They all tend to get increased when you have this extra energy in the atmosphere. I call it being on steroids . . . for the atmosphere."[121] The interviewer asked Masters to explain what he meant, and he extended the metaphor perfectly:

Metaphorical Missiles And Minefields

Well, normally, you have the everyday ups and downs of the weather, but if you pack a little bit of extra punch in there, it's like a baseball hitter who's on steroids.

You expect to see a big home run total maybe from this slugger, but if you add a little bit of extra oomph to his swing by putting him on steroids, now we can have an unprecedented season, a 70 home run season. And that's the way I look at this year.

We had an unprecedented weather year that I don't think would have happened unless we had had an extra bit of energy in the atmosphere due to climate change and global warming.

I put the figure into a headline as a simile—*PBS Covers Link Between 2011's 'Mind-Boggling' Extreme Weather and Global Warming: It's Like 'Being on Steroids'*—and it was retweeted two hundred and fifty times.

FROM THE BIBLE TO BOB DYLAN

Given the power of metaphors, we know we will see and hear them in the best pieces of rhetoric, from antiquity to today. The Bible is the source of many well-known metaphors and similes:

- The Lord is my Shepherd.
- Keep me as the apple of the eye.
- Ye are the salt of the earth.
- The nations are as a drop of a bucket.

Joseph J Romm

Jesus loved metaphors and was a master of word play.
His best known metaphors are about himself, but with
a twist:

- I am the bread of life.
- I am the light of the world.
- I am the gate.
- I am the good shepherd.
- I am the way, the truth and the life.
- I am the vine, you are the branches.

The twist is that these metaphors all begin with "I am"
and we know from Exodus that "I am" is another name
for God: "God said unto Moses, I AM THAT I AM: and
he said, Thus shalt thou say unto the children of Israel,
I AM hath sent me unto you."[122] As we have seen repeatedly, Jesus, a master preacher, is a master of rhetoric
and word play.

Metaphors have never gone out of style, from the
Bible and Shakespeare to modern times. They never
will. Our greatest songs are metaphorical. The best-
selling single since they began charting singles in
the 1950s is built on a simile.[123] Elton John says in his
tribute to Princess Diana (a revision of his tribute to
Marilyn Monroe) that she lived her life "like a candle
in the wind." Lady Gaga's uber-hit "Poker Face" is an
extended metaphor of love as a poker game.

Some similes and metaphors strike such a strong
chord that they become a permanent part of our culture. Here's one that has its origins in the oldest of
proverbs: *A rolling stone gathers no moss.* In 1962, one

of the greatest rock 'n' roll bands of all time formed, the Rolling Stones. They took their name from the song "Rollin' Stone" on a Muddy Waters album they owned.[124]

Three years later, in June 1965, Bob Dylan wrote and recorded his greatest song using the same phrase, but this time as a simile (and inspired by a Hank Williams song).[125] The chorus to Dylan's song is a caustic comment on the life of a woman who has ignored the warnings that she was headed for a fall and who meets her inevitable fate: "How does it feel?" Dylan asks repeatedly, to be homeless, "Like a complete unknown, Like a rolling stone."

Dylan, the bard for the baby boomers, was a student of the stinging simile—"She aches just like a woman, But she breaks just like a little girl"—and here shows that in the hands of a true poet, similes can sometimes have more power than metaphors. After all, the fallen woman is not "a complete unknown" since she was once rich and popular, but she is now worse off: She is "like a complete unknown." Similes can be a potent way to make an ironic point, since they say that you are "like" something, but you aren't *really* that thing.

Ultimately, the most successful music magazine would adopt the metaphor for its title, *Rolling Stone*, cementing it to rock 'n' roll and giving it the kind of permanence that only the best figures of speech achieve. But then this metaphor is unique in that it both comments poignantly on the lifestyle of the modern

Joseph J Romm

rock superstar and reaches back to the millennia-old origins of touring musicians—the wandering minstrel, the traveling troubadour, the pre-Homeric bards—who gave us the oral tradition of poetic lyrics, which led to rhetoric in the first place.

Because metaphors are so potent and so sweeping, not only are they widely used, they are widely misused.

MIXED METAPHORS

The messiest misuse of metaphor is the mixed metaphor, two or more metaphors that are at odds, that fight each other in a foolish fashion—a knight in shining armor trying to wrestle an alligator in a swamp.

The most famous mixed metaphor, the one *Webster's Dictionary* gives as its sole example of a mixed metaphor,[126] comes from Shakespeare—and not just anywhere in Shakespeare but in his most famous speech in his most famous play:

> To be or not to be, that is the question:
>> Whether 'tis nobler in the mind to suffer
>> The slings and arrows of outrageous fortune,
>>> Or to take arms against a sea of troubles,
>>> And by opposing end them?

How can you "take arms against a sea of troubles"? You can't use weapons against the sea. We may ask whether the greatest poet and playwright in the English language, the master of rhetoric, has made a mistake here. Or has he created a subtle visual image of futility? In fact, this speech is the key to decoding the mystery of *Hamlet*: The military metaphor suffusing these five lines is extended throughout the entire play. The mixed metaphor is no mistake. Shakespeare is saying that for Hamlet, taking arms against his troubles would be as futile as taking arms against a sea.

Using a mixed metaphor on purpose to make a point, however powerful, is best left to a master like Shakespeare. In the words of TV stuntmen, "Don't try this at home."

A METAPHOR TOO FAR

Metaphor is the Superman of figures. Metaphors are strong because they directly link two things that are quite distinct. The Lord is your shepherd, the world is a stage, your troubles are a sea. Because metaphors are so all-encompassing and yet leave so much to the imagination, they can cause great controversy.

For instance, Lincoln's famous "A house divided against itself cannot stand" was the strongest possible biblical metaphor, implying that "slavery was doomed according to the word of God," as historian Harold Holzer put it. Yet Lincoln was put on the defensive by Stephen Douglas during their debates because of this metaphor, and the future president lost the 1858 Senate election, perhaps in part because of it. Over the next two years, Lincoln worked hard to "bury his lingering reputation as the radical doomsayer," and the pivotal Cooper Union speech discussed in Chapter Four was filled with shovelfuls of words to do the burying. For instance, Lincoln shifted the origin of his opposition to the spread of slavery from God—our biblical "Father"—to the founding fathers. He repeated the nation's "fathers" thirty times in that 1860 speech, which was crucial to his winning the Republican Party nomination.[127]

During the 2010 midterm election, Sarah Palin "marked with cross hairs" some districts of congressional Democrats "she had targeted for defeat," as the *Washington Post* reported.[128] Arizona Democrat Representative Gabrielle Giffords, "whose district was one of those 20, had publicly complained that this was an invitation to violence." Many argued these cross-hairs were a visual metaphor inciting violence.

When Giffords was later shot, Palin herself came under figurative fire. And she returned fire:

> "Within hours of a tragedy unfolding, journalists and pundits should not manufacture a *blood libel* that serves only to incite the very hatred and violence they purport to condemn. That is reprehensible."

The term "blood libel" was one of the worst metaphorical misfires imaginable: "The phrase refers to a centuries-old anti-Semitic slander—the false charge that Jews use the blood of Christian children for rituals—that has been used as an excuse for persecution." Whether or not Palin understood the full implications of the metaphor, the use of those two words blew up the rest of her message and was widely seen as contributing to her declining poll numbers.

In March 2012, the campaign team of former Massachusetts Gov. Mitt Romney unintentionally launched one of the most powerful negative metaphors imaginable against their own candidate. Romney strategist Eric Fehrnstrom was asked about how his boss's politics might change after he gets the nomination. "I think you hit a reset button for the fall campaign," he said. "Everything changes. It's almost like an Etch-A-Sketch. You can kind of shake it up and we start all over again."

This metaphor erased all the previous metaphors used for Romney's tendency to be on all sides of an issue—like flip-flopper—and drew a simple, compelling visual image that still shadows Romney months later. Why? *Washington Post* columnist Chris Cillizza explained, "Gaffes that matter are those that speak to a larger narrative about a candidate or a doubt/worry that voters already have about that particular candidate." The Etch-A-Sketch gaffe "is likely to linger in the electorate because it speaks to a broader storyline already bouncing around the political world: That Romney lacks any core convictions and that he will say and do whatever it takes to win."[129]

As the columnist Michael Kinsley's defined it, "a gaffe is when a politician tells the truth."

Another reason this is likely to endure is that it is a visual metaphor that everyone knows from childhood. Like all vivid metaphors, it connects something we understand and can describe easily (how an Etch-A-Sketch works) with something we can't (how Romney works). If a picture is worth a thousand words, then a good metaphor is worth two thousand.

Etch-A-Sketch is itself a figure of speech—a rhyme—which makes it an even more memorable phrase. And you can hold it in your hands. It can be used as a prop. Romney's opponents, Rick Santorum and Newt Gingrich, immediately had events holding Etch-A-Sketches. It was too late in the nominating fight to matter to the outcome. But Etch-A-Sketch sales jumped by 1,500 percent, and I saw a member of Congress holding one at a hearing I testified at a few days later.

If team Obama has language intelligence, we'll see and hear a lot about Etch-A-Sketches.

We underestimate the wild and sometimes perverse power of metaphors at our peril. A twenty-two-year-old Churchill put it well:

> The ambition of human beings to extend their knowledge favours the belief that the unknown is only an extension of the known: that the abstract and the concrete are ruled by similar principles: that the finite and the infinite are homogeneous. An apt analogy connects or appears to connect

these distant spheres. It appeals to the everyday knowledge of the hearer and invites him to decide the problems that have baffled his powers of reason by the standard of the nursery and the heart. Argument by analogy leads to conviction rather than to proof, and has often led to glaring error.[130]

Miscast metaphors are minefields.

DYING METAPHORS

In his 1946 essay, "Politics and the English Language," Orwell decries what he calls "dying metaphors." On the one hand, he is a big booster of freshly hatched ones: "A newly invented metaphor assists thought by evoking a visual image." On the other, dead metaphors aren't entirely a no-no: "A metaphor which is technically 'dead' (e.g. *iron resolution*) has in effect reverted to being an ordinary word and can generally be used without loss of vividness." But in between the hatched and the hackneyed is a vast infirmary, a critical care unit where dying metaphors live out their final days, occasionally taken out for a slow walk by lazy writers and speakers whom Orwell disdains.

These dying metaphors "have lost all evocative power and are merely used because they save people the trouble of inventing phrases for themselves." Some of his examples are:

toe the line
ride roughshod over

no axe to grind
Achilles' heel

| stand shoulder to shoulder with | swan song |
| play into the hands of | hotbed |

Thanks to the miracles of modern metaphorical medicine, these have all managed to survive on life support for more than sixty years: They seem as popular as in his time. Orwell points out that "some metaphors now current have been twisted out of their original meaning without those who use them even being aware of the fact." He cites as an example *toe the line*, which, he notes, is "sometimes written as *tow the line*." Just Google those two phrases to find out how common that mistake is going on six decades after Orwell wrote his essay to plead with us to toe the linguistic line.

Orwell's first rule for writers is, "Never use a metaphor, simile, or other figure of speech which you are used to seeing in print."

I have peppered this chapter on metaphor with far too many of them—to illustrate their endless variety. In regular persuasive writing, too many figures are truly like excess pepper, ruining your best thinking. For savory prose, sprinkle metaphors sparingly. But learn to use them well. Modern public speaking is bland and needs more fresh metaphorical spice.

CHAPTER SEVEN
EXTENDED METAPHOR: FRAMING A PICTURE-PERFECT SPEECH

The Lord is my shepherd; I shall not want.
He maketh me to lie down in green pastures:
He leadeth me beside the still waters.
He restoreth my soul:
He leadeth me in the paths of righteousness for his name's
sake.
Yea, though I walk through the valley of the shadow
of death,
I will fear no evil: for thou art with me;
Thy rod and thy staff they comfort me.

—Psalm 23

Extended metaphor is, for me, the most important rhetorical device. This figure is at the heart of some of Lincoln's greatest speeches. It pumps the life blood into Shakespeare's greatest plays. Political candidates with a strong extended metaphor have a long political life while those without one don't have much of a pulse.

Joseph J Romm

Like the best figures, extended metaphors make ideas and phrases more memorable, expanding the vivid visual imagery painted by a single metaphor to create an entire mental mural for the audience. And like the best tropes, which "turn" the meaning of words, extended metaphors force you to think—and in a deeper way than most figures.

Extended metaphors run throughout the Bible. Revelation is almost entirely an extended metaphor or allegory. The psalms are an extended metaphor menagerie, as are Jesus's parables. Jesus takes the most well-known extended metaphor from Psalms, the shepherd metaphor from Psalm 23, which opens this chapter, and extends it into one of his most famous parables:

> I am the good shepherd. The good shepherd lays down his life for the sheep. The hired hand is not the shepherd who owns the sheep. So when he sees the wolf coming, he abandons the sheep and runs away. Then the wolf attacks the flock and scatters it. The man runs away because he is a hired hand and cares nothing for the sheep. I am the good shepherd; I know my sheep and my sheep know me—just as the Father knows me and I know the Father—and I lay down my life for the sheep.

One best-selling Elizabethan text uses an extended metaphor to explain that while a simple metaphor "may be compared to a star in respect of beauty, brightness and direction," an extended metaphor may be

Extended Metaphor

"fully likened to a figure compounded of many stars . . . which we may call a constellation."

No wonder this figure is so widely used. Who wouldn't want to have their words achieve the impact and longevity of heavenly images like the Big Dipper or Orion?

LADY GAGA AND EXTENDED METAPHORS

Extended metaphors are not the exclusive domain of Scripture. Popular poets and song-writers inevitably turn to them for storytelling.

The top-selling song of 2009, Lady Gaga's "Poker Face," which has been viewed online more than one hundred million times, is an extended metaphor of love as a game of poker and chance:

> I wanna hold 'em like they do in Texas, please.
> Fold 'em, let 'em hit me, raise it, baby, stay with me
> (I love it).
> Luck and intuition play the cards with spades to start
> And after he's been hooked I'll play the one that's on his heart.

Later verses compare love to a dice game and Russian roulette, but the main point of the extended metaphor is that Gaga has a poker face—the man can't read her true feelings. Indeed, Gaga has said the point of the song is that she "used to fantasize about women when I was with my boyfriend."

The song is full of puns, another figure of speech. The punning use of "hold 'em" and "heart" here is topped by the title, "poker face," which is to say, "poke her face," but I'll leave this racier discussion for Chapter Eight. This is a song of seduction, as the chorus makes clear: "I'll get him hot, show him what I've got" though, as we will see, it is really aimed at seducing the listener or viewer, with the help of the figures of speech.

Another monster hit, "Bad Romance," is also an extended metaphor—love as a bad romance novel or film. As the chorus states: "I want your love, And I want your revenge. You and me could write a bad romance."

The song runs through the metaphors of romance fiction (good and bad):

> I want your drama. . . .
> I want your leather-studded kiss in the sand. . . .
> I want your horror. . . .
> I want your *Psycho*
> Your *Vertigo* shtick
> Want you in my *Rear Window*

Those last three are references to Alfred Hitchcock classics—with the last two punning double entrendres. Most online lyric sheets have the line as "your vertical stick"!

This particular extended metaphor was, as of June 2012, the fourth most watched YouTube video of all time, with more than 460 million views. In 2011, Lady

Gaga explained her song-writing philosophy: "I just like really aggressive metaphors—harder, thicker, darker and my fans do as well."[131]

LINCOLN AND EXTENDED METAPHOR

To explore why extended metaphors have come to be so important in modern politics, let's begin with Lincoln's masterful use of them. In the Gettysburg Address, Lincoln gives us a subtle but powerful example. Lincoln makes this two-hundred-and-seventy-word speech unforgettable using an extended metaphor of birth, death, and resurrection to increase the coherence and impact of his brief remarks.

From the very beginning, Lincoln delivers a variety of references to birth, "Fourscore and seven years ago our *fathers brought forth* on this continent a *new* nation, *conceived* in liberty and dedicated to the proposition that all men are *created* equal."[132] He says the civil war is testing whether "any nation so *conceived* . . . can long endure."

Lincoln then moves on to images and words of death, as befits the horrific battlefield in front of him, with phrases such as "*a final resting-place* for those who here *gave their lives*" and "the brave men, living and *dead*" and "these honored *dead*" and "these *dead.*"

Finally, he returns to the original metaphor of birth, but with a twist: We must resolve that "this nation under God shall have a *new birth* of freedom, and that government of the people, by the people, for the people *shall not perish* from the earth."

Birth, death, rebirth, and immortality ("shall not perish")—in a place that we will make sacred ("hallow" and "consecrate" and the key repeated word, "dedicate")—is a stunning extended metaphor that turns into a biblical allusion of hope for transcendence even during the worst suffering. The Battle of Gettysburg has become a symbolic national crucifixion. Winston Churchill termed Lincoln's speech "the ultimate expression of the majesty of Shakespeare's language."

Extended metaphors are often far more overt, as in Lincoln's "house divided" speech at the start of his Illinois Senate race against Stephen Douglas. Lincoln describes how the combined effect of Supreme Court decisions and policies by Douglas and others was to extend slavery into new territories in spite of local opposition. Lincoln said "we can not absolutely know" that Douglas and the others were working together to achieve this effect, "But when we see a lot of framed timbers, different portions of which we know have been gotten out at different times and places, and by different workmen . . . and when we see these timbers joined together, and see they exactly matte the frame of a house" then it is "impossible not to believe" that everyone "worked upon a common plan or draft drawn up before the first blow was struck."

Stephen Douglas resented Lincoln's implication in the "House Divided" speech that he was part of a conspiracy to extend slavery, a charge and a metaphor Lincoln never tired of repeating everywhere. In his famous debates with Lincoln, Douglas responded with a harsh figure of his own—sarcasm:

> He [Lincoln] studied that out—prepared that one sentence with the greatest care, committed it to memory, and put it in his first Springfield speech, and now he carries that speech around and reads that sentence to show how pretty it is. His vanity is wounded because I will not go into that beautiful figure of his about the building of a house. All I have to say is, that I am not green enough to let him make a charge which he acknowledges he does not know to be true, and then take up my time in answering it, when I know it to be false and nobody else knows it to be true.

But Lincoln had thought through the implications of his figure. He would not give it up, as Lincoln scholar Roy Basler has explained: "Under the implications of Lincoln's figure, constantly pressed, Douglas was constrained to make a statement of opinion that, although it immediately cleared his way in the senatorial contest, eventually cost him the presidency."[133]

Why was Lincoln so fond of extended metaphors? They are certainly common figures in the Bible and Shakespeare, including his favorite speech in *Hamlet*. We know Lincoln knew of the figure, since "allegory," which "may be regarded as a metaphor continued," is one of the fourteen figures of speech discussed in

Joseph J Romm

Kirkham's *English Grammar,* the book Lincoln studied from age twenty-three. [134] I suspect that the reason he liked the figure is the same reason that modern candidates do: It is a masterful means of framing a political debate, exactly as he crafted the framed-timbers-of-the-house extended metaphor to frame Douglas for the crime of extending slavery.

Politicians with language intelligence, like Lincoln, repeat and extend their metaphors.

REAGAN AND EXTENDED METAPHORS

Extended metaphors are essential to politics for several reasons. First, as we've seen, they are a key to great speechmaking. Second, we humans think with extended metaphors. So the best politicians naturally present themselves to fit our metaphors, linking those metaphors to their personal story, feeding the modern media's growing interest in personalities and dramatic stories. Third, the best way to attack your opponent's positive extended metaphor is to hit back with a negative extended metaphor. Put another way, rhetoric is the art of creating a persuasive story, the art of making—and unmaking—an emotional connection with voters.

Before exploring the theory, let's look at classic examples. In 1984, the Reagan campaign team realized the American public was making political decisions in a more personal way and that how a politician framed an issue could be as important as which side of the issue they came down on. The team came out with two of the most memorable TV ads in the history of American politics. One of the ads became a major theme for Reagan, "It's morning again in America" (with the visual of a day starting for working America). This metaphor perfectly captured Reagan's optimism.[135]

Another famous ad showed a grizzly bear, the symbol of Russia, as the narrator said:

> There is a bear in the woods. For some people the bear is easy to see. Others don't see it at all. Some people say the bear is tame. Others say it's vicious and dangerous. Since no one can really be sure who is right, isn't it smart to be as strong as the bear? If there is a bear.

Short words, repetition and antithesis, along with a sweeping extended metaphor: Russia is the bear, Reagan sees the bear for what it is, and his massive military buildup is a smart response, whereas his Democratic challenger, Walter Mondale, is presumably the one who either doesn't see it or thinks it is tame. The final line—"If there is a bear"—is pure irony, since the ad starts by saying there is a bear, and we the audience actually see the bear. The whole point of the figures is to make words and ideas stick in the mind. This ad is the essence of rhetoric distilled to thirty seconds.

Reagan loved extended metaphors. The one he used the most was "politics as sports." Reagan himself played football at Eureka College, and in the movie *Knute Rockne: All-American*, he played George Gipp—

who dies at age twenty-five, days before being named Notre Dame's first All-American Football Player. The catchphrase, "Win one for the Gipper," is one Reagan and his supporters repeated often.[136] Here is an extended metaphor from his reelection stump speech delivered in various forms in the fall of 1984:

> We all watched the Olympics, and we saw our athletes go for the gold. Well, there are two teams in America today. There's the Washington tax increase team and the grassroots opportunity team. Now, making the economy bear the burden of our opponents tax hike would be like having some of those Olympic swimmers their coach telling them that they had to swim while carrying an anvil [laughter] or a runner would sprint with a ball and chain [laughter]. And that's what Coach Tax Hike and his tax increase team want to do [laughter] and they kicked off their campaign with that call this year. And they said it was a kickoff; I think it was a fumble [laughter].
>
> . . . And come November, the American people are going to decide which team is America's team and, come November, I just can't help but believe the American people are going to tell 'Coach Tax Hike' and the whole tax increase team to head for the showers.[137]

In November of that year, Reagan scored the most lopsided electoral victory in US presidential history, 525 to 13, a score never seen in an actual football game.

Extended Metaphor

POLITICS AS WAR

Considerable psychological and linguistic research has been done in the past few decades on how people think. George Lakoff and Mark Johnson describe one major conclusion of that research in their book, *Metaphors We Live By*: "We have found . . . that metaphor is pervasive in everyday life, not just in language but in thought and action. Our ordinary conceptual system, in terms of which we both think and act, is fundamentally metaphorical in nature."[138]

We now know that extended metaphors frame thinking in politics, law, science, religion, and language itself. One of Lakoff's key points is that dozens of metaphors are "reflected in our everyday language by a wide variety of expressions." He lists these for the *argument is war* metaphor:

> Your claims are *indefensible.*
> He *attacked every weak point* in my argument.
> His criticisms were *right on target.*
> You disagree? OK, *shoot!*
> If you use that *strategy,* he'll *wipe you out.*
> He *shot down* all my arguments.

Argument-is-war is an extended metaphor that pervades our language and thinking, one that extends back centuries. One best-selling Elizabethan author describes the figures of speech as "martial instruments both of defence & invasion." Lincoln explained that the figures of speech "are weapons which hit you, but miss us." Churchill labeled analogy and metaphor "among the most formidable weapons of the rhetorician." For masters of rhetoric, like Lincoln and Churchill, their verbal battles were a kind of warfare because the stakes were so high. As Kennedy said of Churchill, "He mobilized the English language and sent it into battle" during World War II.[139]

To reverse the most famous line of the nineteenth-century's leading military theorist, Carl von Clausewitz, let's define politics as a continuation of war by different means, by means of rhetoric. The argument-is-war metaphor, I think, helps people rationalize in their own minds the use of the strongest possible tactics.

Harsh verbal tactics have become the norm in political campaigns, epitomized by the brutal but brilliantly false Swift Boat ads. The media are complicit in this coarsening because they are either allies in repeating any attack no matter how baseless or because they are appeasers who ignore the attacks. Perhaps they do one evenhanded story while the nightly verbal carpet-bombing continues unabated, rendering that one well-reported story largely irrelevant.

Because the media loves to highlight the drama of politics, and few things are more dramatic than warfare, the media adores the "politics is war" metaphor. Here are quotes from each of the three major networks evening news shows on just one September night during the highly combative 1996 presidential campaign.

Extended Metaphor

ABC's Peter Jennings said, "The president is going to come under further Republican attack." CBS's Dan Rather said, "Bob Dole re-opened one of his favorite lines of attack today about President Clinton's health records." NBC's Tom Brokaw actually mixed his boxing and military metaphors:

> Bob Dole on the ropes and looking for a way to boost his sagging campaign made it clear today he is taking off the gloves in the war of the political airwaves.[140]

Brokaw's words show how all the metaphors merge into one: Politics is sports is war.

We have reached a tragic nadir where all of the weapons of rhetoric appear to be completely fair game: There is rarely a public penalty for using the most potent verbal tactic in politics even when based on lies. More than ever, politicians who do not master rhetoric, who do not have language intelligence, are defenseless against those who do. To come full circle, politicians who successfully create a negative image of their opponent are described using a linguistic metaphor: Clinton "defined" Dole in 1996, tying him to Newt Gingrich and labeling him a mean-spirited obstructionist. Bush "defined" Kerry as a flip-flopper.

Rhetoric was discovered and developed by the Greeks and Romans in part to help them win debates. Modern debates are also won by those who are smarter about using rhetoric. In particular, the key to beating your opponent in a televised debate, or the equally important post-debate spin, is to find and repeat endlessly a sound bite from the debate that fits the *negative* extended metaphor you are creating for that opponent.

This was the strategy used by the Bush team to trample Al Gore in the pivotal first debate during the 2000 campaign. In that campaign, a key Bush metaphor was that he wasn't the publicly humiliated adulterer of infinite tongue, Bill Clinton. He was then, much as he was through 2004, the blunt, trip-over-his-own tongue, regular guy, committed to "restoring honor and dignity to the White House," as British journalist Martin Lewis has written.[141] Gore distanced himself from the president, refusing to let Clinton campaign; choosing for his running mate Senator Joe Lieberman, a religious and moralistic man who had publicly criticized Clinton's behavior; and famously kissing his wife, Tipper, at the end of his acceptance speech. All this helped put Gore into the lead going into the first presidential debate.

But the Bush team better understood how strategy and rhetoric work together, how to create a successful extended political metaphor. As Lewis explained, the Bush team came up with a plan to "take all of Gore's perceived weaknesses and find a way to characterize them as all being part of the same character flaw. And the kicker was that it would be the self same defect that the public had detected in Clinton." Now *that* is extending a metaphor.

Extended Metaphor

The Republicans had long mocked Gore for perceived exaggerations, tainting him with twisted or out-of-context versions of various claims, such as his statements that he had taken the initiative on legislation that created the internet (which, in fact, he had). For the first debate, Bush's opposition research team established a "massive database of every utterance in Gore's 26 years in public service," and waited for him to make a slight misstatement. In a BBC interview, Tim Griffin, the GOP's deputy head of research, explained the value of opposition research with our favorite war metaphor: "Research is a fundamental point. We think of ourselves as the creators of the ammunition in a war. Research digs up the ammunition. . . . We make the bullets."[142]

Griffin extended the metaphor with a sign he erected in the Bush team's War Room, the term for the rapid response headquarters James Carville set up for Clinton in 1992 that was popularized in the movie of the same name. The sign read: "On my command—unleash hell on Al." This quote, minus the "on Al," came from the blockbuster movie of that year, *Gladiator*. It was uttered by General Maximus (Russell Crowe) before the Roman legions launched their massive firepower on the barbarian hordes.

When Gore said, incorrectly, that he visited fire sites in Texas with FEMA Director James Lee Witt, the Bush team opened fire. As one GOP opposition researcher put the spin, "The man can't tell the truth. He uses legalisms and he parses words just like his master, Bill Clinton, to get out of trouble." Lewis writes, "The *New York Post* trumpets LIAR LIAR on its front page— and the post-debate spin cycle becomes about Gore's perceived chronic character flaw." This is especially impressive political spin given that Gore did visit fire sites in Texas with a different FEMA executive, and at other times he had visited Texas with Witt. To be effective, an extended metaphor in politics doesn't have to be entirely true, especially if your opponent fails to fight back effectively.

Even with all the rhetorical advantage, Bush still lost the popular vote to Gore and almost lost the election itself. If his campaign team had had only slightly more language intelligence, Al Gore might well have become president.

FRAMING THE POLITICAL DEBATE

The best, most successful political campaigns create two extended metaphors: They paint themselves with a positive one and smear their opponent with a negative one. Losing campaigns either have no extended metaphor or they mix their metaphors.

Look at the 2004 presidential campaign. The Democrats never had a clear metaphor to label Bush with. They never had a coherent view of Bush. On the one hand, we were repeatedly told Bush was a liar, that he had deceived us into going to war with Iraq, lied about the weapons of mass destruction, lied about the connection between Saddam Hussein and Osama Bin Laden, and so on. On the other hand, we were given the image from Michael Moore's *Fahrenheit 9/11* of Bush sitting in a Florida schoolroom listening to someone read the children's book *My Pet Goat* for several minutes the morning of September 11, 2001, even after learning that the United States was under attack. The movie ended with Bush fumbling over an old adage, "Fool me once, shame on . . . shame on you. Fool me . . . you can't get fooled again."

But if he's a dunce, can he also be a liar? If he's a puppet, how can he also be a puppeteer? How can he be a fool and also be fooling us? The Democratic team and its allies never understood Bush's strategy, so they never got that the Bush-as-idiot message didn't hurt the president and may have helped him, may in fact have perfectly fit into his eiron image discussed in Chapter Four. Many of the ads by the Democrats and their allies probably canceled each other out.

The attempt to present Kerry as a viable military leader in 2004 on the basis of his Vietnam record (the metaphor of "band of brothers" and "reporting for duty") was shot down by the endlessly repeated Swift Boat ads, although they were almost entirely false. Kerry's Dukakis-like failure to defend himself at once undercut his own metaphor by underscoring an extended metaphor of weakness commonly applied to Democrats: They are wimps who are easy to bully and just aren't tough enough. Put another way, if Kerry can't defend himself, how can he defend America? This is the kind of irony that the public has come to expect, as we've seen, and which is fatal to presidential candidates.

Also, Kerry's metaphor was not extended: He steadfastly refused to link his Vietnam record to his position on Iraq. Had he done so, he might have taken his seemingly incoherent votes—*for* the war but *against* the money to run the war—and painted a picture of consistency: As with Vietnam, he had supported the war to begin with, but then when he saw how it was run in an incompetent and self-defeating manner, he had to speak out against it to save lives. *Extended metaphors force you to weave a simple and consistent story out of your principles, your record, and your future plans*, which Kerry never did.

The Bush team, on the other hand, had a clear metaphor for Kerry—the flip-flopper, which was nice alliteration as well as a verbal and visual metaphor that they repeated and extended at every chance. The true power of the flip-flop metaphor is its subtext: Someone who flip-flops, someone who is inconstant, must perforce lack guiding principles and values. In short, he's not like us, and he can't be trusted. The Bush team's ad showing Kerry windsurfing in one direction and then the next was thus a metaphorical two-fer: Kerry changes direction like the wind, and regular folks don't windsurf.

Extended Metaphor

In 2008, the public wanted change after eight years of Bush. Barack Obama and Hillary Clinton each had a big advantage: They were both powerful visual metaphors for change since neither of them looked like any of the previous presidents. Obama understood this was a change election, and his entire message was built around change, including his simple slogan: "Change we can believe in." In that sense, he had a fully consistent extended metaphor or narrative. In contrast, Hillary Clinton ran as an establishment candidate—the safer choice, the one who could handle a 3:00 a.m. phone call. This fundamental incoherence of message was one of many mistakes that cost her the nomination.

In the general election, Sen. John McCain's campaign suffered from almost the exact same incoherent narrative. On the one hand, he tried to present himself as the steady hand, the war veteran who was more experienced than the young freshman senator from Illinois. But McCain also tried to paint himself as a "maverick" who would bring change to Washington. His bold gamble to pick Sarah Palin, an unknown governor from Alaska, was meant to highlight his maverick credentials.

You can run as a maverick change agent or you can run as an experienced, establishment, steady hand. But you can't do both and tell a consistent story. Worse, media interviews made Palin appear as a risky choice to be a heartbeat from the presidency. When McCain briefly suspended his campaign during the financial crisis, he just reinforced the extended metaphor that the Obama campaign had for him as "erratic." McCain/Palin became a risky choice.

It is particularly unusual for a candidate to repeatedly define himself in a negative fashion, but that appears to be what Mitt Romney did in winning the Republican presidential nomination. In a series of off-the-cuff remarks, the former governor and businessman, who is worth a quarter-billion dollars, became the stereotypical out-of-touch rich guy:

- "Corporations are people, my friend."
- "I like being able to fire people who provide services to me."
- "I know what it's like to worry whether you're going to get fired."
- "I'm not concerned about the very poor."
- "Ann [his wife] drives a couple of Cadillacs, actually."
- "I have some great friends who are NASCAR team owners."
- "I'm also unemployed."

Each one by itself is a modest gaffe. Collectively, they are a self-made, self-defeating narrative.

Romney is one of the worst communicators in recent memory to win any party's presidential nomination. *Politico* talked to "thirty different Republican leaders across the country" about Romney, and Executive Editor Jim VandeHei reported on June 5, 2012 that "they are so nervous that he'll improvise rhetorically, which got him into a lot of trouble in the primary."[143]

Extended Metaphor

NPR reported in April 2012 on "a disastrous speech" Romney gave in a nearly empty football stadium before the Michigan primary.[144] NPR noted the speech was criticized because it "sounded like a mushy rehash of things he had already rolled out." The reporter asked who wrote the speech. The reply: "After some hemming and hawing, the senior advisors sort of rolled their eyes and said the governor wrote the speech, meaning Romney wrote it." If he lacks the language intelligence to speak off-the-cuff or write his own speeches, Romney had better find a very good logographos if he wants to reframe his narrative.

The power of frames and extended metaphors—the reason why smart orators use them—is that they cannot be overturned merely by presenting contrary facts. Let me repeat that: Facts cannot fight false frames. You must fight metaphorical fire with metaphorical fire.

"One of the fundamental findings of cognitive science is that people think in terms of frames and metaphors," writes linguist Lakoff. "The frames are in the synapses of our brains, physically present in the form of neural circuitry." In recent decades, linguists, cognitive scientists, and others have shown how frames and extended metaphors are at the heart of how we think about "our most important abstract philosophical concepts, including time, causation, morality, and the mind." Countless books and articles underscore that extended metaphors are at the core of all human thinking.[145]

Here is the key lesson for politics from cognitive science, as Lakoff puts it: "When the facts don't fit the frames, the frames are kept and the facts are ignored."

The identical conclusion was reached by Royal Dutch Shell's top strategic planners. Even though these planners foresaw the energy crisis of the 1970s and presented the results to Shell's management, "no more than a third of Shell's critical decision centers" were acting on the insights gained from the energy crisis scenario, noted Pierre Wack, one of the planners. Wack came to realize that although all managers had the new information, most were still processing it through their old paradigm or mental model, what Wack called their "microcosm."

> I cannot overemphasize this point: Unless the corporate microcosm changes, managerial behavior will not change; the internal compass must be recalibrated. . . .
> Our real target was the microcosms of our decision makers: unless we influenced the mental image, the picture of reality held by critical decision makers, our scenarios would be like water on stone.[146]

Simply pointing out the flaws in a scientific theory or in a manager's worldview or in the public's perception of a candidate's policy and moral framework is never useful—none of these will change their thinking or their behavior or their voting. In popular terms, "You can't beat a horse with no horse."

Extended Metaphor

The systematic application of rhetoric is one of the few ways to create a worldview—what more profound paradigm is there in America than the Judeo-Christian ethic as created and sustained in the supreme rhetoric text, the Bible? In the beginning was the Word. Similarly, the systematic application of rhetoric is one of the few ways to destroy a worldview, as is understood by the best campaign strategists.

If you cannot change the public's worldview, microcosm, paradigm, extended metaphor, or frame, then you cannot change how they perceive the facts. This is especially problematic in our time, a time when people can easily choose to watch only those media outlets that share their political views and thus pre-filter facts for them. The clearest evidence of this trend was the sobering October 2004 report, "The Separate Realities of Bush and Kerry Supporters."[147] The report found:

> A large majority of Bush supporters believe that, before the war, Iraq had weapons of mass destruction or a major program for building them . . . and that this was the conclusion of the recently released report by Charles Duelfer. A large majority of Bush supporters believes that Iraq was providing substantial support to al Qaeda and that clear evidence of this support has been found. A large majority believes that most experts also have this view, and a substantial majority believe that this was the conclusion of the 9/11 Commission. Large majorities of Kerry supporters believe the opposite on all these points.

That the Bush voters' beliefs were also at odds with the facts is strong testimony to the ascendancy of both the alternative media and rhetoric. A Zogby poll found that "a whopping 86% of Bush voters watch the Fox Network most often for news."[148] It was also, I would argue, testimony to the Democratic Party's poor messaging capability, which is to say poor language intelligence, which is to say poor understanding of rhetoric.

The Democrats have again and again had inapt messages, inept messaging, and inopportune messengers. One can hardly imagine a worse phrase to build a major policy campaign around than "public option"—except maybe "cap-and-trade." Both of these phrases focus on process, on policies never fully explained to the public, rather than on outcomes the public desires—secure healthcare coverage or lower pollution.

I'm not suggesting that bad messaging is the only failing of the Democrats. Far from it—they have made many policy mistakes, too. But I do believe that until a person or a political group fixes its messaging, until it acquires language intelligence, it simply has little chance of enduring success.

One of the best-known progressive columnists, E.J. Dionne, wrote in January 2010 about Obama's failure to develop a coherent message:

> Yet the truth that liberals and Obama must grapple with is that they have failed so far to dent the right's narrative, especially among those moderates and

independents with no strong commitments to either side in this fight.

The president's supporters comfort themselves that Obama's numbers will improve as the economy gets better. This is a form of intellectual complacency. Ronald Reagan's numbers went down during a slump, too. But even when he was in the doldrums, Reagan was laying the groundwork for a critique of liberalism that held sway in American politics long after he left office.

Progressives will never reach their own Morning in America unless they use the Gipper's method to offer their own critique of the conservatism he helped make dominant.[149]

The new media reality means it will be increasingly difficult for either party to win over the other party's voters. So the ability to use rhetoric, one of the few ways known to successfully attack someone's belief system, will only grow in importance. And the debates will take on even greater prominence in presidential politics, as they represent one of the only times candidates get to address a large fraction of the voters unfiltered while at the same time having an opportunity to directly attack their opponent's extended metaphor.

Extended metaphor remains the most important of rhetorical devices.

CHAPTER EIGHT

THE FIGURES OF SEDUCTION

My advice, then, young men of Rome, is to learn the noble
Advocate's arts—not only to let you defend
Some trembling client: A woman, no less than the populace,
Elite Senator, or grave judge,
Will surrender to eloquence. Nevertheless, dissemble
Your powers, avoid long words,
Don't look too highbrow.

—Ovid, *The Art of Love*[150]

Rhetoric has a dark side. Rhetoric can manipulate, misdirect, and mislead. Dissembling salespeople use rhetoric to persuade us to surrender our money. Dissembling politicians use rhetoric to persuade us to delay action on global warming, to unwittingly surrender our children's future. The language intelligence needed to thwart those ultra-subtle and ultra-sophisticated seducers comes naturally to very few. To be resisted and debunked, their verbal tricks must be made explicit, which is the goal of this chapter.

The dark side of rhetoric was well-known—and well-feared—in ancient Greece. The term "Sophists" originally applied to those who taught rhetoric (and other subjects) for pay. The Sophist Protagorus boasted he could make the weaker cause appear to be the stronger. Hence *sophistry*, the term for disingenuous arguments.

In his dialogue *Gorgias*, about the master rhetorician, Plato gives him a speech that dramatizes the awesome power of rhetoric:

> If a rhetorician and a doctor visited any city you like to name and they had to contend in argument before the Assembly or any other gathering as to which of the two should be chosen as doctor, the doctor would be nowhere, but the man who could speak would be chosen, if he so wished.[151]

So a rhetorician could persuade any audience, no matter how intelligent, that he was more of a doctor than a real doctor. No wonder climate science deniers, skilled in the art of verbal persuasion, can out-debate a scientist.

Cicero describes the birth of rhetoric's evil twin in *De Inventione*: "But when a certain . . . depraved imitation of virtue . . . acquired the power of eloquence unaccompanied by any consideration of moral duty, then low cunning supported by talent began to corrupt cities and undermine the lives of men."[152] That's a chillingly accurate description of Shakespeare's Iago and other seducers.

Rhetoric's power was recognized by intellectuals and audiences in Shakespeare's day. In the words of one scholar, Elizabethan rhetoricians repeatedly "celebrate rhetoric for giving its possessor the ability to subjugate others."[153]

Shakespeare was drawn to seducers. He made them central characters, as in the case of Iago and Marc Antony. He gave them his full range of verbal skills and the power to manipulate his other characters. No one has so expertly and explicitly combined all the figures of seduction as Shakespeare.

RHETORICAL SEDUCTION TODAY

You may not believe that you are under daily assault from those who would seduce you, who would manipulate you with the most subtle and insidious tricks. Believe it.

To find the dazzling array of devices used to manipulate you by salespeople, read Kevin Hogan's books *The Psychology of Persuasion* (1996) and *The Science of Influence* (2004). Hogan promises readers in his 2004 book, "I'm going to show you the ins and outs of *permanent* change in other people's behavior, why it's difficult—and how you can go about making it happen. You want the customer for life? It's here."[154]

Find Frank Luntz's "Straight Talk" memo online and read his deplorable advice to Republicans on how to use language to delay action on fighting global warming. Read Luntz's memo published before the health-care reform debate of 2009, which the Republicans followed closely, to great success. Read the 2010 book *Merchants of Doubt: How a Handful of Scientists Obscured the Truth on Issues from Tobacco Smoke to Global Warming,* which explains how so many have been neatly seduced into inaction on climate change using the same rhetorical tactics developed by tobacco companies to delay smoking regulations.

THE FIGURES OF SEDUCTION

The figures of speech move us by design. They were modeled after the words and phrases that touch us emotionally. As we've seen, modern social science research reveals that the figures make words and ideas more memorable, that our brains are wired to respond to the figures, and that the figures reflect the way we think. We think metaphorically. As one best-selling Elizabethan author put it over five hundred years ago:

> By the great might of figures (which is no other thing than wisdom speaking eloquently), the orator may lead his hearers which way he lists, and draw them to what affection he will; he may make them to be angry, to be pleased, to laugh, to weep, and lament; to love, to abhor, and loathe; to hope, to fear, to covet; to be satisfied, to envy, to have pity and compassion; to marvel, to believe, to repent; and briefly to be moved with any affection that shall serve best for his purpose.[155]

That is to say, the basic figures of speech can be used to seduce us, to cause us to take actions that harm us or others. But to persuade moral people to do immoral things, a seducer will also use words whose intended meaning is different from their literal meaning. This looks very much like a job for irony, and indeed many of the figures of seduction are closely related to irony.

Seduction, like persuasion, is a two-step dance for a master of rhetoric. First, a seducer must convince you that he or she is a trustworthy person, a person who shares your values and speaks your language. This is the first strategy for all orators, as Aristotle explained more than two thousand years ago. But since seducers are trying to lead you astray, they must necessarily deceive. Ovid advised the young men of Rome who wanted to seduce women to "dissemble your powers, avoid long words, don't look too highbrow." This may sound familiar, since it is the strategy of the *eiron*, which comes from the Greek for "dissembler," as discussed in Chapter Four. Marc Antony, Iago, and Hal/Henry V all practice this precise strategy.

Once a would-be seducer has established he is trustworthy, that he is a plainspoken, straight-shooting person who means what he says and says what he means, then he can safely start saying what he doesn't mean.

INDIRECT SUGGESTION

One of the most powerful figures of seduction, and certainly the most ironic, is the indirect suggestion.

Very popular with rhetoricians and Shakespearean seducers, this device was rediscovered in the twentieth century by the founders of NLP, neuro-linguistic programming. The creators of NLP systematically modeled the most effective techniques of therapeutic persuasion and suggestion, particularly the work of Milton Erickson.

The basic idea of indirect suggestion is that if you want to move people to do something they have a resistance to, one approach is to state the idea indirectly, even in the negative. In his 1996 book on persuasion, Kevin Hogan gives the following examples of what to say to a possible but reluctant customer:[156]

- "Don't feel as though you have to buy something today."
- "Don't decide now."
- "Don't make up your mind too quickly."
- "You probably already know that you're going to buy this."
- "I could tell you that you are making a mistake but I won't."

The first reason this works is that the negating words (like "don't" or "won't") do not stick in the mind as much as the positive ideas or images that follow them. As George Lakoff explains in his 2004 book, *Don't Think of an Elephant!*, if I say that to you, you will think of an elephant.

In one 1990 study, undergraduate students observed sugar from a labeled commercial container as it was poured into two bottles.[157] They then labeled one bottle "sugar" and the other "not sodium cyanide." Students avoided eating sugar from the second bottle even though they had watched it being poured and "even though *they* had arbitrarily placed that label on it" and knew the label was accurate—that it was *not* sodium cyanide. Such is the power of words or, rather, the insidious lack of power of the word *not*.

Even more insidious, "when people find a claim familiar because of prior exposure but do not recall the original context or source of the claim, they tend to think that the claim is true," noted a 2005 journal article, "How Warnings about False Claims Become Recommendations."[158] You must understand this point to debunk those who spread disinformation, as we'll see.

The second reason this trick works is that the speaker is not telling you what to think. Quite the opposite. The speaker can appear to be on your side, seeming to warn you against an idea or a course of action, all the while carefully planting in your mind the very idea he or she claims to be negating.

The therapists who developed this strategy were not trying to seduce people or lead them astray, but rather were trying to overcome the resistance their patients had to changing their behavior. These behavior patterns were deeply ingrained over many years and thus not easy for patients to change consciously, even when they were made aware of how counterproductive

Joseph J Romm

the behaviors were. So the therapists developed strategies for helping their patients change.

You may not believe in indirect suggestion. But those
who developed rhetoric did. The Greeks called this *apophasis* (from the Greek word for "to deny"), the figure of
speech that emphasizes a point by pretending to deny it,
that stresses an idea or image by negating it. I am labeling apophasis one of the powerful figures of seduction.

For me, the most compelling two reasons to believe in the power of this figure is, first, Shakespeare
believed in it, and, second, he knew his audiences did,
too. His plays openly reveal what so many have tried to
keep hidden.

LEND ME YOUR EARS

The play *Julius Caesar* is explicitly about seduction.
Cassius, he of the "lean and hungry look," has assem-
bled a group of conspirators to assassinate Caesar. To
add credibility to the proposed assassination, Cassius
seduces the noble idealist Brutus—highly respected
throughout Rome—into joining them, though Brutus
turns out to require only modest persuasion. Cassius
even says of Brutus, *"For who so firm that cannot be seduced?"* This is the motto of all seducers: Who is so
firm that they cannot be seduced? Anyone can be led
astray—any of us, all of us.

After Brutus, Cassius, and the other conspirators
murder Caesar, Brutus speaks to the citizens in the

forum and convinces them the assassination was justified. How can Marc Antony turn Brutus's words against
him and convince the Romans that Brutus did not act
honorably in killing Caesar? He does it with good old-
fashioned verbal irony, as we have seen. And it is no
surprise that Antony also uses the ironic figure of apophasis. Antony and Shakespeare wield the figures with
more devious skill than had ever been seen before on
stage.

Antony's primary goal is to enrage the citizens to
"mutiny," so he uses the word three times, stressing it
each time by pretending to deny it. First, Antony says
he would be doing wrong to the conspirators "if I were
disposed to stir your hearts and minds to *mutiny* and
rage." He puts the idea in the conditional, using *if*.
Second, Antony says, "Sweet friends, let me not stir you
up to such a sudden flood of *mutiny*." He puts the idea
in the negative, using *not*. Here is apophasis directly.
Third, Antony says he is not an orator like Brutus, but
if he were Brutus, he would give a speech that would
"move the stones of Rome to rise and *mutiny*." What
is particularly remarkable, in our efforts to divine
Shakespeare's rhetorical technique, is what he wrote
for the very next line:

All: We'll *mutiny*.

In other words, directly after Antony plants the idea
of *mutiny* in their minds through three conditional and
negative statements, directly after he ends his speech
with the embedded suggestion *rise and mutiny*, all the

Roman citizens shout the word, adopting it as their plan of action.

Antony criticizes the citizens for failing to mourn for Caesar: "O judgment! Thou art fled to brutish beasts, and men have lost their reason." This is another classic verbal trick, using a word that sounds very similar to one that you want someone else to think of. Antony wants the citizens to associate the word *Brutus* with the word *brutish*, with beasts that lack reason. He wants to negate the idea that Brutus is either honorable or reasonable. He succeeds.

He wants the citizens to lose *their* reason. He tells us he must not read Caesar's will to them because "It will inflame you, it will make you mad." This is apophasis. To make sure we understand that the citizens have lost their reason, Shakespeare inserts a short scene after Antony's speech in which a mob of citizens slaughter an innocent poet just because he has the same name as one of the conspirators—Cinna. Madness rules.

Shakespeare expected his audience would follow what he was doing in this scene, having Antony use every classical rhetorical device for indirect suggestion to plant ideas in the unconscious minds of the Roman citizens. The best proof that Shakespeare did this intentionally is that he does it in all his great plays, including *Othello*.

We fail to learn from Shakespeare's wisdom at our own peril.

MODERN APHOPHASIS

Determining whether someone is using this devious device today is not always easy. We often use the phrasing of apophasis, pretended denial, without intentionally trying to plant ideas or manipulate people. Indeed, mild forms of apophasis are such a common language pattern in politics that they barely qualify as seduction. For instance, on New Year's Day 2011, former Massachusetts governor Mitt Romney said of his rivals for the GOP presidential nomination:

> "Like Speaker Gingrich, **Sen. Santorum has spent his career in the government, in Washington. Nothing wrong with that.** But it's a very different background than I have, and I think that the people of this country recognize with our economy as the major issue we face right now, it would be helpful to have someone who understands the economy firsthand, who's spent the bulk of his career working in the private sector."[159]

Obviously, Romney intends to leave people with the idea that there is something wrong with being a career politician—otherwise, why mention it? Indeed, it is widely seen as a negative label and had been the subject of an earlier back-and-forth between Gingrich and Romney. Here the line isn't fooling anyone. It's just Romney's way of pretending he's not engaging in a negative attack.

Joseph J Romm

The Iraq war provides numerous examples of more sophisticated use of pretended denial and indirect suggestion. For instance, a key aspect of the Bush Administration's justification for war was that Iraq possessed weapons of mass destruction, which in turn made Saddam Hussein a unique threat we could no longer ignore. As one analyst explained in 2004, "Under international law, specifically under the U.N. Charter, one nation may go to war with another only in self-defense; pre-emptive action only constitutes self-defense when an imminent danger to a country's security can be demonstrated."[160]

In January 2004, ten months after the war began, White House press secretary Scott McClellan said that the issue of the failure to find weapons of mass destruction was not important because the administration had never said Iraq was an immediate threat. He said, "I think some in the media have chosen to use the word 'imminent'. Those were not words we used."[161]

The principals had generally been too clever, using apophasis and indirect suggestion. In November 2002, Secretary of Defense Donald Rumsfeld said:

> "I would look you in the eye and I would say, go back before September 11 and ask yourself this question: Was the attack that took place on September 11 an *imminent threat* the month before or two months before or three months before or six months before? When did the attack on September 11 become an *imminent threat?* Now, transport your-

> self forward a year, two years or a week or a month.
> . . . So the question is, when is it such an *immediate*
> *threat* that you must do something?"[162]

These lines would make eiron Marc Antony proud. Rumsfeld managed to fashion a reputation for himself as a "plain blunt man" like Antony, and he wields words as skillfully as any Greek rhetorician. Rumsfeld is particularly good at asking questions that he then answers: "Is it [post-war Iraq] going to be as efficient as a dictatorship? No. Is it going to be vastly more desirable? You bet."[163] It should be no surprise to learn this is also a figure of speech (*anthypophora*).

Note that in the lines quoted above, Rumsfeld beats the drum on September 11 three times and seemingly links Iraq and September 11, but only seemingly. And he thrice repeats the phrase "imminent threat" or "immediate threat" without ever directly calling Iraq one.

In his January 2003 State of the Union address, Bush matched his secretary of defense. He gives a lengthy description of all of the various weapons of mass destruction that Saddam Hussein was supposed to have, although, as we learned much later, he didn't. Bush says, "The only possible explanation, the only possible use he could have for those weapons, is to dominate, intimidate or attack." Then he continues:

> And this Congress and the American people must
> recognize *another threat.* Evidence from intelligence
> sources, secret communications and statements by

people now in custody reveal that Saddam Hussein aids and protects terrorists, including members of Al Qaida. Secretly, and without fingerprints, he could provide one of his hidden weapons to terrorists, or help them develop their own.

Before September the 11th, many in the world believed that Saddam Hussein could be contained. But chemical agents, lethal viruses and shadowy terrorist networks are not easily contained.

Imagine those 19 hijackers with other weapons and other plans—this time armed by Saddam Hussein. It would take one vial, one canister, one crate slipped into this country to bring a day of horror like none we have ever known.

We will do everything in our power to make sure that that day never comes.

Some have said we must not act until the threat is imminent. Since when have terrorists and tyrants announced their intentions, politely putting us on notice before they strike?[164]

Impressive. He linked Al Qaida and September 11 to Saddam Hussein again and again. He sums up with the pithy alliterative phrase "terrorists and tyrants." As we know from the 9/11 Commission Report, there was no actual link between 9/11 and Saddam Hussein, beyond the linguistic link you can make by mentioning them in the same sentence and connecting them with the word "and." The administration knew this but nevertheless took every opportunity to make the link anyway, which is no doubt why so many of the people who voted for Bush thought there was a link. Like Rumsfeld, Bush made a vivid appeal to the listener's imagination, in this case to visualize the hijackers armed by Saddam Hussein. As psychologists know, that which we can visualize, we are more likely to believe.

The italicized line above is an advanced form of apophasis where the pretended denial is put in the mouth of an imaginary third party, "Some have said." It allows Bush to say "the threat is imminent" without actually saying it. What would a typical listener take away from all this? Here's how one highly informed listener, Maura Reynolds of the *L.A Times*, heard the speech:

BUSH CALLS IRAQ IMMINENT THREAT

By Maura Reynolds

WASHINGTON—A somber and steely President Bush . . . provided a forceful and detailed denunciation of Iraq, promising new evidence that Saddam Hussein's regime poses an imminent danger to the world and demanding the United Nations convene in just one week to consider the threat....

Calls have mounted in recent weeks for the president to make a better case for going to war. In response, Bush argued that use of force is not only justified but necessary, and that the threat is not only real but imminent.[165]

That is how the story was heard by a news reporter whose business is words and clarity, who could write her story with a copy of the speech in front of her. Imagine how the general public would hear the speech.

The Bush team appears to have wanted to create the impression of an imminent threat while maintaining what might be called "rhetorical deniability" that they ever used the specific word "imminent" themselves. After all, Bush had spoken of the "unique and urgent threat posed by Iraq" in November 2002.[166] And the administration had worked hard to create a similar rhetorical deniability that they ever said Saddam Hussein was behind 9/11, even though they clearly wanted to create the impression the two were directly connected.

Is this seduction? When you use devious rhetorical devices to intentionally mislead, that is the definition of seduction. Is all this intentional? Your answer no doubt depends on your politics. For me it strains credulity to think that these wizards of word usage have done this unintentionally when they have so brilliantly used every other element in the periodic table of rhetoric. Scott McLellan himself later accused President Bush of pursuing a "propaganda campaign to sell the war to the American people," as he wrote in his 2008 book *What Happened: Inside the Bush White House and Washington's Culture of Deception*, which *Politico* labeled a "surprisingly scathing memoir."[167]

Apophasis works. You should keep your eyes—and ears—open for it, especially if someone is trying to sell you something when the pitch is emotional, and a wrong decision could be costly.

We should all minimize the use of negative suggestions in everyday life. For example, avoid saying to your children things like "Don't whine" but instead say "Use your normal voice." Similarly, when you make an important phone call to someone who is busy, don't ask, "Are you busy?" or, "Is this a bad time to talk?" as the words "busy" and "bad time" will ring in their ears. Ask, "Is this a good time to talk?"

Finally, understanding apophasis is crucial for those in the business of debunking myths, as I am. The 2005 study "How Warnings about False Claims Become Recommendations" concluded:

> **Telling people that a consumer claim is false can make them misremember it as true.** In two experiments, older adults were especially susceptible to this "illusion of truth" effect. Repeatedly identifying a claim as false helped older adults remember it as false in the short term but paradoxically made them more likely to remember it as true after a 3 day delay. This unintended effect of repetition comes from increased familiarity with the claim itself but decreased recollection of the claim's original context. Findings provide insight into susceptibility over time to memory distortions and exploitation via repetition of claims in media and advertising.[168]

When the Centers for Disease Control and Prevention put out a flier to debunk myths about the flu vaccine, it repeated several myths, such as, "The side effects are worse than the flu" and labeled them false. A study of people given the flier found that "within 30 minutes, older people misremembered 28 percent of the false statements as true." Worse, "three days later, they remembered 40 percent of the myths as factual." And they identified the source of their erroneous beliefs as the CDC itself. As explained in a 2007 *Washington Post* article, "Persistence of Myths Could Alter Public Policy Approach": "Indeed, repetition seems to be a key culprit. Things that are repeated often become more accessible in memory, and one of the brain's subconscious rules of thumb is that easily recalled things are true."[169] This, of course, is precisely why repetition is so important for persuasion, why rhetoric has some four dozen figures of repetition.

A 2004 journal article, "'I am not guilty' vs 'I am innocent'," found that for many people, the "negation tag" of a denial falls off with time:

> "If someone says, 'I did not harass her,' I associate the idea of harassment with this person," said [lead author Ruth] Mayo, explaining why people who are accused of something but are later proved innocent find their reputations remain tarnished. "Even if he is innocent, this is what is activated when I hear this person's name again. If you think 9/11 and Iraq, this is your association, this is what comes in your mind," she added. "Even if you say it is not true, you will eventually have this connection with Saddam Hussein and 9/11."

The authors found that rather than deny a false claim, it is better to make a completely new assertion that makes no reference to the original myth. It takes a lot of message discipline to do this, but if you want to debunk a myth, you need to focus on stating the truth, not repeating the myth.

Accidental use of apophasis has always been one of the most common mistakes speakers make, even the most experienced. Richard Nixon said, "I am not a crook," and only his final word still rings in our ears.

MORE FIGURES OF SEDUCTION

Two other figures of seduction are closely related to apophasis and embedded suggestion. The first is *aposiopesis* (from the Greek "becoming silent"), an abrupt breaking off of speech. A two-thousand-year-old Latin textbook on rhetoric and persuasion writes of this technique, "A suspicion, unexpressed, becomes more telling than a detailed explanation would have been." It gives an example: "He who so handsome and so young, recently at a stranger's house—I am unwilling to say more."[170]

An Elizabethan author warns of aposiopesis, "If it be used in malice, it commonly leaves the venom of some false suspicion behind it, all which faults are in wisdom and charity to be eschewed." Simply pausing in one's remarks, "becoming silent," raises suspicions that all is not what it seems.[171]

The second figure is *paralipsis*, passing over a subject briefly to create an ominous suggestion about what is not being said. The Latin textbook gives an example: "Your boyhood, indeed, which you dedicated to intemperance of all kinds, I would discuss, if I thought this the right time. But at present I advisedly leave that aside." The Roman author cautions, "This figure is most abused by malice, as when it is applied in false accusation."[172]

The master of both these techniques is, no surprise, the master of false suspicion and false accusation: Iago. He wields these weapons best in the "temptation scene," Act Three, Scene Three of *Othello*, called "perhaps the most breath-taking scene in the whole of Shakespeare."[173]

Iago's goal is to poison Othello's mind, to seduce him into believing that his lieutenant, Cassio, has been having an affair with his wife, Desdemona. Iago starts slyly and slowly, just after Cassio departs from a meeting with Desdemona (that Iago had set up):

Iago	Ha, I like not that.
Othello	What dost thou say?
Iago	Nothing, my lord; or if—I know not what.
Othello	Was not that Cassio parted from my wife?
Iago	Cassio, my lord? No, sure, I cannot think it That he would steal away so guilty-like Seeing you coming.

The Figures Of Seduction

Here we have all the tricks in one place. In a single sentence he manages to combine the pretended omission of paralipsis ("Nothing, my lord") with the sudden breaking off of aposiopesis ("or if—I know not what"). He then follows quickly with his own brand of apophasis ("I cannot think . . .") to introduce the suggestion that Cassio would "steal away so guilty-like" upon seeing Othello coming. This scene may be the best dramatization of the dark side of rhetoric ever written.

Modern day eirons use these tricks because they are playing dumb. They gloss over a subject quickly to draw their victims' interest. Con artists, for instance, let some rich mark overhear a scheme, and then when the mark asks for more information, they say, "I really can't talk about this." TV cops use paralipsis all the time. Lieutenant Columbo's favorite phrase, "Just one more thing," was a variation, where he made the most important thing he wanted a suspect to hear seem like an afterthought that almost escaped his mind entirely. Or he'd bring up a series of insinuations until the person he is talking to demands to know, "What's your point, Lieutenant?" to which his reply is, "Point? No, no. No point."[174]

My favorite political aposiopesis occurred in the final presidential debate of the 2004 election during an exchange on healthcare:

> KERRY: Well, two leading national news networks
> have both said the president's characterization of

165

> my healthcare plan is incorrect. One called it fiction. The other called it untrue. . . .
> BUSH: In all due respect, I'm not so sure it's credible to quote leading news organizations about—oh, never mind.[175]

The president abruptly cut off his attack on the credibility of the mainstream media. The beauty of this aposiopesis is that Bush's remark sent a strong message to his supporters, who don't like the media, but because he did not finish his sentence, most of the media didn't treat it as a fully completed thought about Bush's dismal view of them. Thus the line was hardly subjected to the same kind of scrutiny that every other line in the debate was. As one puzzled blogger wrote, "I listened hard afterward to commentators on CNN, MSNBC, NPR and Fox and not one mentioned this very strange moment."[176] Had the president completed his sentence, then the remark might well have become the subject of widespread scrutiny and perhaps scorn.

The aposiopesis allowed him to speak to his supporters and to all those who are skeptical of the media—and no one else. This has long been seen as one of the aims of rhetoric: dividing people into groups (those who are in the know and those who aren't) and targeting your message. Was this intentional on the president's part or did he really think better of finishing his sentence in the spur of the moment? We can't know, but either the example shows it is a powerful rhetorical device or it shows how the figures of speech do, in fact, capture the essence of real emotions and real speech patterns.

ENIGMA

> *There are certain common privileges of a writer, the benefit whereof, I hope, there will be no reason to doubt; particularly, that where I'm not understood, it shall be concluded, that something very useful and profound is couched underneath; and again, that whatever word or sentence is printed in a different character shall be judged to contain something extraordinary either of wit or sublime.*

—Jonathan Swift[177]

Clarity is rightly seen as one of the most important virtues of a speech. If our goal is to persuade people honestly, then we should be as clear as possible about what we are trying to say. Clarity is most important when we are trying to convince people with the facts, with logic. As we've seen, however, truly persuasive speech requires a simultaneous appeal to mind and heart, logic *and* emotion, especially if you are trying to penetrate and change someone's worldview.

Aristotle and others writers on rhetoric argued that making a persuasive emotional appeal means sounding genuinely emotional yourself. But emotional people often do not speak with clarity. They omit words, they misuse words, they don't speak smoothly, they make mistakes. The craftiest of orators have long recognized this. In his treatise *On Style*, the ancient Greek rhetorician Demetrius explained that "loose word-arrangement" can make one sound more forceful, and cites as an example the orator Hipponax: "When he wants to attack his enemies he breaks his rhythm, makes it halting instead of straightforward, less rhythmical, and this suits the forcefulness of his attack."[178]

Lack of clarity has also been seen as a rhetorical strategy. There are actually a number of closely related "figures of obscuring." One such figure is *enigma* (from the Greek for "riddle"), which is deliberately "obscuring one's meaning," or using speech where "the sense may hardly be gathered." Another is *schematismus*, which is using figurative language to conceal a meaning, either because it would be unsafe or indecent to "speak directly and openly." A third figure of obscuring is *noema*, the "figure of close conceit" (from the Greek word for "understanding"), which might best be described as speech that is unclear to one group of listeners but clear to another. It is used "to conceal the sense from the common capacity of the hearers: and to make it private to the wiser sort, who by a deep consideration of the saying, are best able to find out the meaning." Examples of enigma and noema are given below.[179]

Why would a rhetorician want to be intentionally confusing or enigmatic? One reason is to send a message that would be clear to one group of people but not to another. This is noema, a private message to those "best able to find out the meaning." To use a modern metaphor, this is called "dog-whistle politics," referring to the device that emits a high pitch only dogs can hear—hence any message "only fully audible to those at whom it is directly aimed," as the *Economist* put it in 2005.[180]

Bush's chief speechwriter, Michael Gerson, an evangelical Christian who had at one point been a theology major in college, seeded Bush's speeches with words meaningful to the religious but innocuous to others, including *whirlwind, work of mercy, safely home, wonderworking power*. This is noema, courtesy of a master logographos. Biblical scholar Bruce Lincoln explains that Bush's October 7, 2001, speech announcing the war in Afghanistan had allusions to Revelation, Isaiah, and the gospels. By the end of the speech, "America's adversaries have been redefined as enemies of God, and current events have been constituted as confirmation of Scripture," Lincoln notes. "Bush could only make these points indirectly, through strategies of double coding." Bush's speech had a surface meaning for secular listeners and a deeper meaning for the devout. [181]

A second reason you might choose to be enigmatic is to appear more profound, as Swift wrote slyly in the quote that opens this section, to stimulate your audience's interest, its craving for answers to the myriad mysteries of life. Poets have always employed obscure language for this purpose. Modern-day bards, especially lyricists, are very fond of this technique, which is why the lyrics to so many songs are never fully explained.

John Lennon and Paul McCartney repeatedly use allegory and enigmatic phrasing in songs like "I Am the Walrus," "Lucy in the Sky with Diamonds," and "Norwegian Wood," to name but a few. Countless explanations have been offered for the lyrics of what is surely the longest allegorical pop song ever written, "American Pie" by Don McLean, as McLean no doubt expected and desired ("The jester sang for the king and queen in a coat he borrowed from James Dean").[182]

Then there is the jester himself, Bob Dylan, singing, in McLean's allegorical words, with "a voice that came from you and me." Dylan's masterpiece, "Like a Rolling Stone," is filled with enigmatic expressions such as "the mystery tramp" and "Napoleon in rags" and "You used to ride on the chrome horse with your diplomat."

The mysterious words help connect us with the main lyric "How do you feel?" by conveying the confusion of the life of Miss Lonely, the once too-proud woman now brought low. Ever the jester, Dylan offered comments on his song that sum up the ultimate meaning to be found in *enigma*:

> Anybody can be specific and obvious. . . . That's always been the easy way. . . . It's not that it's so difficult to be unspecific and less obvious; it's just that there is nothing, absolutely nothing, to be specific and obvious *about*. My older songs, to say the least,

were about nothing. The newer ones are about the same nothing—only as seen inside a bigger thing, perhaps called nowhere.[183]

LADY GAGA'S POKER FACE

Who could be more of an enigma than someone with a poker face? Lady Gaga's monster hit "Poker Face" repeats the title phrase thirty times, repeats the phrase "he can't read my poker face" ten times, and throws in the phrase "can't read my" another twenty times to make sure no one misses the point. Not surprisingly, then, the song has multiple layers of seduction and enigma in it.

Gaga is seducing the man, as this repeated line makes clear: "I'll get him hot, show him what I've got." That is one of the many gambling puns or double entendres in this extended metaphor of love as a game of poker and chance. In poker, if you are called in the final round of betting, you have to show your cards at the end. The music video builds on that metaphor by turning the game of Texas hold 'em into strip poker where most of the participants show most of what they've got by the end.

On the surface, the point of the song is that the man can't read her true feelings. She has a poker face. The deeper meaning is that Gaga "used to fantasize about women when I was with my boyfriend."[184] Gaga is famously non-traditional, non-heterosexual, like much of her fan base, so the multiple layers of meaning allow her to appeal to multiple audiences.

The song contains the rhetoric-filled line, "I won't tell you that I love you, kiss or hug you, 'Cause I'm bluffin' with my muffin." Here "muffin" is a sexual reference, so this metaphorically restates the theme that she is deceiving the man and would rather be with a woman. This deeper meaning would appear to be no-ema, since it was clearly lost on some of her listeners, which became clear after Kanye West took Gaga's vocals from an acoustic version of "Poker Face" to make his own song. MTV interviewed Gaga about the song:

> "It's funny, because a lot of my fans were like, 'Gaga, Kanye wrote a song . . . and it's not about what your record's about. Your record is about gambling. And this song is about dirty sex things'. . . .
> "I said to them, 'You're wrong. Kanye was right,'" she laughed. "That's exactly what this song is about."

It's not clear to me how listeners could have missed the sexual references, but obviously Gaga appeals to a great many young and very literal fans. MTV described Gaga's revelation this way: "Kanye broke her musical Da Vinci Code."

In fact, West revealed yet a deeper seductive element of the song—and the real reason why Gaga used the poker metaphor. He heard the line as "I poke her face." In its entry on "poke her face," The *Urban Dictionary* goes so far as to say, "The song subliminally advocates oral sex by repeating the phrase poke-her-face" multiple times.[185]

Wikipedia notes of West's non-subliminal piece, "The song was originally entitled 'I Poke Her Face' but was changed to make it more acceptable for radio." Gaga is much subtler and more enigmatic than West, who is in-your-face, figuratively and literally. No doubt Gaga's ability to appeal to, to seduce, multiple audiences with multiple layers of meaning using multiple figures of speech has contributed to her stunning success.

CONCLUSION

I have often seriously debated with myself
whether men and communities have received more
good or evil
from oratory and a consuming devotion to eloquence.

—Cicero[186]

Rhetoric can't tell you *what* to say in a headline, tweet, slogan, witticism, story, or speech—only *how* to say it in a wowing and winning way.

Rhetoric is the art of persuasion, the systematic use of the figures of speech. Mastery of rhetoric is critical to explaining the enduring power of Shakespeare and the King James Bible. Rhetoric is the scaffolding of Lincoln's and Churchill's most brilliant oratorical constructions. President Obama has largely ignored rhetoric and narrative during his presidency—and suffered the consequences.

Language intelligence does not explain all the success of the great persuaders, but try to imagine any one of them *without* language intelligence or rhetorical skill. We would probably not even remember their names. Language intelligence is the key to creating and sustaining a memorable brand for a product or a person.

Jesus was the Word, logos—rhetoric made flesh. Shakespeare turned rhetoric into flesh-and-blood characters. Rhetoric can explain every line of the mystery that is *Hamlet*—but that is the subject of another book.

My goal has been to help you become more persuasive and less seducible. If you have already begun to speak differently and listen differently after reading this book, then I have succeeded. If you are wittier on Twitter and have headier headlines, then I have succeeded.

If facts were sufficient to persuade people, then experts in science would rule the world. But facts are not, and scientists do not.

We filter out all the facts that do not match our views. We all have filtering worldviews (extended metaphors or frames) through which we view the world. These worldviews are the source of most of our judgments and intuitions and decision-making—from picking mates to picking products to picking candidates. Penetrating someone's worldview—and, for the best rhetoricians, replacing it with a different one—requires a systematic approach: rhetoric. As Plato put it, rhetoric is "the art of winning the soul by discourse."

Conclusion

To sum up the key rhetorical strategies used by the greatest persuaders:

1. Use short, simple words.
2. Repeat, repeat, repeat. Repetition is the essential element of all persuasion.
3. Master irony and foreshadowing. They are central elements of popular culture, modern politics, and mass media for a reason—they help us make sense of the stories of our lives and other people's lives.
4. Use metaphors to paint a picture, to connect what your listeners already know to what you want them to know. Metaphors may be the most important figure as well as the most underused and misused.
5. Create an extended metaphor when you have a big task at hand, like framing a picture-perfect speech or launching a major campaign.
6. If you want to avoid being seduced, learn the figures of seduction. If you want to debunk a myth, do not repeat that myth.

Language intelligence and mastery of rhetoric do not come from a list. On the other hand, you can't get the dawn-to-dusk, thirty-six-weeks-a-year, year-in-and-year-out immersion in each and every figure that Shakespeare and the King James translators received in grammar school. Twenty-five centuries of wisdom and experience have been largely ignored by teachers and students of all ages and all disciplines, even those most dependent on eloquence. Many law schools don't even offer elective courses in rhetoric.

It's as if MIT trained its physics students without calculus. The century-old words of Winston Churchill are truer than ever: "The subtle art of combining the various elements that separately mean nothing and collectively mean so much in an harmonious proportion is known to a very few."

If you want to learn rhetoric, if you want to boost your language intelligence, you will have to master these basic strategies to the point where they become your natural way of speaking. You can do it—it's why I wrote this book. Lincoln, America's greatest rhetorician, was self-taught. So was Bob Dylan, the baby boomer's bountiful bard.

Dylan used a quarry's worth of figures in his song, "Like a Rolling Stone"—repetition, metaphor, irony, enigma, and, of course, the stinging rhetorical question, "How does it feel?" Why? To do what rhetoric does best: involve us in the song *emotionally*. Dylan wants us to feel what he feels—contempt for the pride and hubris of Miss Lonely.

Dylan achieved his mastery of rhetoric by studying the Bible, the great song lyricists, and the great poets. He visited the New York Public Library again and again to read newspapers articles from before the Civil War. He was "intrigued by the language and rhetoric of the times." Are you ready to be as diligent as Dylan?

As a child, Lady Gaga listened to Michael Jackson, The Rolling Stones, and the Beatles on her plastic tape recorder over and over again. She was raised Catholic

Conclusion

and went to a Catholic girls school. She wrote her first piano ballad at thirteen and was performing open mike at fourteen. At seventeen, she went to New York University's Tisch School of the Arts to study music and songwriting. In 2011, she explained why her songs are so metaphorical: "I just like really aggressive metaphors . . . and my fans do as well."

If you can be meaningful, the figures can make you memorable. Indeed, rhetoric can make you memorable even if you don't have much to say.

I have tried to identify the best, most compelling examples of all the figures. If you have been persuaded here that rhetoric is worth studying, then you already know the best textbooks for further study. Even those who are not religious should study the Bible religiously. Rhetoric is the godly way of speaking—one reason that those schooled in the Bible tend to have language intelligence. Get an audio tape of the King James version to experience the logos from the most rhetorically brilliant translators. Listen to the best lyricists and study song-writing along with your Bible, and you might make people go Gaga, too.

We can all learn from Lincoln that Shakespeare's great speeches are worth memorizing and that his plays, especially the great tragedies and histories, are worth rereading many times and hearing live in the theater. I recommend starting with *Julius Caesar* and then going on to *Hamlet* and *Othello*.

Joseph J Romm

For the underlying structure of rhetoric, we probably cannot surpass the textbooks that Shakespeare likely used, by Erasmus, John Hoskins, Henry Peacham, and Thomas Wilson. Links to all of the great speeches I have discussed can be found on my (other) website, Rhetoric.com, as can Churchill's insightful 1897 essay, "The Scaffolding of Rhetoric."

The best strategy for attaining eloquence? Take every opportunity to speak in public and use the figures in everyday conversations, blog posts, and tweets. See which ones work for you and which ones don't. Listen closely to those who seek to persuade you, so you can avoid being manipulated, seduced, or bamboozled.

As Thomas Wilson wrote during Shakespeare's time: "What maketh the lawyer to have such utterance? Practice. What maketh the preacher to speak so roundly? Practice. . . . Therefore in all faculties diligent practice and earnest exercise are the only things that make men prove excellent."[187]

AFTERWORD

While everyone can benefit from studying the figures and mastering the basic strategies laid out in this book, I do hope that one group in particular does. My final reason for writing this book is to help scientists and environmentalists and other climate science advocates learn how to harness the power of rhetoric at least as well as those spreading disinformation have.

The nation and the planet face the harsh reality of serious global warming and the irreversible consequences of catastrophic climate change. The rhetorical seduction of global warming denial is built upon a foundation created by the tobacco industry and funded by the fossil fuel industries. It has spread throughout conservative think tanks, the Tea Party, and the conservative message machine. This seduction has been met with messaging failure by the scientific and environmental communities, and progressive politicians.

I have written briefly about the rhetorical failings of climate scientists throughout the book and at even greater length on my blog, ClimateProgress.org.

Back in 2005, the physicist Mark Bowen wrote about glaciologist Lonnie Thompson: "Scientists have an annoying habit of backing off when they're asked to make a plain statement, and climatologists tend to be worse than most." The good news, if you can call it that, is that the climate situation has become so dire that even the most reticent climatologists are starting to speak more bluntly. By the end of 2010, Thompson was writing:

> Climatologists, like other scientists, tend to be a stolid group. We are not given to theatrical rantings about falling skies. Most of us are far more comfortable in our laboratories or gathering data in the field than we are giving interviews to journalists or speaking before Congressional committees. Why then are climatologists speaking out about the dangers of global warming? The answer is that virtually all of us are now convinced that global warming poses a clear and present danger to civilization.

That warning seems pretty clear. Sadly, the White House itself has muddied the message.

Obama Administration sources have told me that the White House Office of Science and Technology Policy wanted to launch a robust defense of climate science in the face of these phony attacks, but the White House communications shop shut them down. At the same time, the White House (and many environmentalists and many of their allies in Congress) tried to sell a bill to address global warming—without actually talking about global warming.[188] In the end, a modest climate plan that was business-friendly and market-oriented got smeared over and over again as big government "cap-and-tax" by conservatives, even though many of them had supported this very idea just two years earlier. Indeed, it was George W. Bush's father who had, two decades ago, actually embraced this approach to environmental problems and gained broad bipartisan support for it. That would be an ironic story, but now it is bordering on tragic.

"In our time, political speech and writing are largely the defense of the indefensible," wrote George Orwell. "Political language . . . is designed to make lies sound truthful and murder respectable, and to give an appearance of solidity to pure wind."[189] Little has changed in the six decades since Orwell wrote "Politics and the English Language."

I did not write this book expecting to end the debasement of political language, but rather to give rhetorical ammunition to those fighting the good fight in the face of the fiercest foes.

ACKNOWLEDGMENTS

I owe a permanent debt to my parents for sharing with me their unmatched language intelligence. I would not have been able to write this book were it not for the guidance and wisdom of my mother, Ethel Grodzins Romm.

I have worked on this book for more than two decades, since my essay "Why Hamlet Dies" was published in the journal *Hamlet Studies* in 1988. In that time countless editors and others have read the book. While I can't name them all here, I took every last piece of criticism to heart, and this book is the better for all of them.

I am particularly grateful to Van Jones for pushing me to publish this book. The incisive comments of Gloria Loomis were instrumental in getting me to trim this book down and eliminate the vestiges of earlier books that were lurking on almost every page. Bill McKibben put me in touch with Gloria and for that I am in his debt.

I thank John Podesta for believing in the idea of ClimateProgress.org and making it possible back in

2006. I am very grateful to the Center for American Progress Action Fund for its ongoing support of the blog. The blog has allowed me to test many of the ideas in this book and get instant feedback from some of the best commenters in the blogosphere. Of course there would be no blog without readers, so I owe all of them a huge debt.

I greatly appreciate the work of the CreateSpace project team in making the process of turning my manuscript into a book so straightforward.

Special thanks go to my wife, Patricia Sinicropi, for supporting my seemingly constant work on the blog and this book. And words cannot describe my gratitude for the gift of my daughter, Antonia, who every day provides me unlimited inspiration. It is Antonias around the world whom we must all bear in mind when we try to communicate how urgent climate action is.

BAD ROMANCE

Acknowledgments

POKER FACE

LIKE A ROLLING STONE

ENDNOTES

All references to Shakespeare plays (unless otherwise specified) follow the act, scene, and line numbers of *The Riverside Shakespeare*, textual editor, G. Blakemore Evans (Boston: Houghton Mifflin, 1974).

All references to the Bible (unless otherwise specified) follow the King James Version available online at http://www.hti.umich. edu/index-all.html.

---

1   Winston Churchill, "The Scaffolding of Rhetoric," unpublished essay, 1897,
    http://www-adm.pdx.edu/user/frinq/pluralst/churspek. htm.
2   This book focuses primarily on English-language rhetoric and rhetoricians.
3   Kennedy was quoting Edward R. Murrow. http:// en.wikiquote.org/wiki/Edward_R._Murrow.
    William H. Herndon and Jesse W. Weik, *Herndon's Life of Lincoln* (New York: Da Capo Press, Inc., 1983 republication of 1942 edition), p. 325.
4   Dante Alighieri, *The Convivio of Dante Alighieri,* (London: J. M. Dent, 1903), p. 117.

Joseph J Romm

5   Henry Peacham, *The Garden of Eloquence* (1593), (Gainseville, FL: Scholars' Facimilies & Reprints, 1954), from the "Epistle Dedicatorie."

6   Monica Moses, "Readers Consume What They See," *Poynter*, August 17, 2002, updated March 2, 2011 http://www.poynter.org/uncategorized/1875/readers-consume-what-they-see/.

7   Raymond W. Gibbs, Jr., *The Poetics of Mind* (Cambridge, UK: Cambridge University Press, 1994), p. 1.

8   "Some Definitions of Rhetoric," http://www.stanford.edu/dept/english/courses/sites/lunsford/pages/defs.htm

9   Jeremy Peters, "At *Newsweek*, a Humble and Frugal Tina Brown," *New York Times*, February 20, 2011

10 Homer, *The Odyssey*, VIII, 166-173, as cited in Brian Vickers, *Classical Rhetoric in English Poetry* (Carbondale: Southern Illinois University Press: 1989), p. 17.

11 George Kennedy, *The Art of Persuasion in Greece* (Princeton: Princeton University Press, 1963), pp. 57-58, 63.

12 Aristotle, *Rhetoric*, as cited in Vickers, *Classical Rhetoric in English Poetry*, p. 94.

13 Churchill, "The Scaffolding of Rhetoric."

14 The definitive work on Shakespeare's knowledge of rhetoric is T. W. Baldwin, *Shakespere's Small Latine & Lesse Greek* (sic), Volumes 1 and 2 (Urbana: University Of Illinois Press, 1944), which devotes fifteen hundred pages to the subject. As Baldwin concludes (Vol. 2, p. 378): "William Shakespere was trained in the heroic age of grammar school rhetoric in England, and he shows knowledge of the complete system, in its most heroic proportions. He shows a grasp of the theory as presented by the various texts through Quintilian. He shows a corresponding grasp upon all the different compositional forms of prose for

Endnotes

which the theory prepared. And this is true whether or not Shakespere ever went to school a day. Manifestly, the sensible thing to do is to permit him to complete Stratford grammar school, as there is every reason to believe that he did."

15 Vickers, *Classical Rhetoric in English Poetry*, pp. 47-48.

16 Vickers, p. 48.

17 Benson Bobrick, *Wide as the Waters: The Story of the English Bible and the Revolution it Inspired* (New York: Simon & Schuster, 2001), pp. 218-219. Bobrick, like many, misunderstands rhetoric, thinking it must require large words, and he writes of these sermons, "But for Andrewes, eloquence was not the point."

18 Harold Holzer, *Lincoln at Cooper Union* (New York: Simon & Schuster, 2004), pp. 5, 285.

19 Ronald C. White, Jr., *The Eloquent President* (New York: Random House, 2005), pp. 102-104; William Scott, *Lessons in Elocution* (Baltimore: Warner & Hann, 1809); Samuel Kirkham, *English Grammar in Familiar Lectures* (New York: Robert B. Collins, 1829).

20 Scott, *Lessons in Elocution*, p. 387. Scott misquotes Shakespeare, dropping "before their deaths."

21 See "Lincoln and Shakespeare," in Roy P. Basler, *A Touchstone for Greatness* (Westport, CT: Greenwood Press, 1973), pp. 206-227. The debate was over which word should be emphasized in the phrase "mainly thrust at me"—'mainly' or 'me.'

22 McGrath, *In the Beginning: The Story of the King James Bible and How It Changed a Nation, a Language, and a Culture* (New York: Anchor Books, 2001), p. 254.

23 Edward F. McQuarrie and David Glen Mick, "On Resonance: A Critical Pluralistic Inquiry into Advertising Rhetoric," *Journal of Consumer Research*, September 1992, pp. 180-197.

24 James H. Leigh, "The Use Of Figures Of Speech In Print Ad Headlines," *Journal of Advertising*, Vol. XXIII, No. 2 (June 1994), pp. 17-33.

25 Roderick Hart, *The Sound of Leadership* (Chicago: The University Of Chicago Press, 1987), p. 46.

26 Jeffrey Tulis, *The Rhetorical Presidency* (Princeton: Princeton University Press, 1987), p. 89.

27 Lincoln's speech is from *The Collected Works of Abraham Lincoln*, ed. Roy Basler, 9 vols. (New Brunswick, NJ: Rutgers University Press, 1953-1955), Vol. 4, p. 210, as cited in Tulis, p. 5.

28 Tulis, p. 186. Ironically, Tulis's book on the "rhetorical presidency" has no discussion whatsoever of rhetoric itself.

29 Quoted in William Schneider, "Marketing Iraq: Why now," September 12, 2002, http://archives.cnn.com/2002/ALLPOLITICS/09/12/schneider.iraq.

30 Mike Allen and Jim Vandehei, "Social Security Push to Tap the GOP Faithful, *Washington Post*, January 14, 2005, p. A06

31 Ezra Klein, "The Unpersuaded," *The New Yorker*, March 19, 2012, http://www.newyorker.com/reporting/2012/03/19/120319fa_fact_klein?currentPage=all

32 Howard Fineman, "The 'Media Party' is Over," January 13, 2005, http://www.msnbc.msn.com/id/6813945/.

33 Pew Research Center, Trends 2005, "Media: More Voices, Less Credibility," p. 49, http://pewresearch.org/assets/files/trends2005-media.pdf "Poll: News Media's Credibility Plunges," CBS News, September 14, 2009, http://www.cbsnews.com/stories/2009/09/14/business/main5309240.shtml

34 The Luntz Research Companies, "Straight Talk,"http://www.ewg.org/files/LuntzResearch_environment.pdf.

Endnotes

35 Ruth Marcus, "Obama's 'Where's Waldo?' presidency," *Washinton Post*, March 2, 2011,
http://www.washingtonpost.com/wp-dyn/content/article/2011/03/01/AR2011030105489.html

36 George Gascoigne, *Certayne Notes of Instruction Concerning the Making of Verse or Rhyme in English*, 1575, quoted in Russ McDonald, *Shakespeare and the Arts of Language* (Oxford: Oxford University Press, 2001) p. 15.

37 Churchill, "The Scaffolding of Rhetoric."

38 Thomas Wilson, *The Art of Rhetoric* (1560), Peter E. Medine, ed. (University Park, PA: Pennsylvania State University Press, 1994), p. 47.

39 Alister McGrath, *In the Beginning*, p. 263

40 "The *Rolling Stone* 500 Greatest Songs of All Time," *Rolling Stone*, November 19, 2004,
http://www.scribd.com/doc/11793203/Rolling-Stone-500-Greatest-Songs-of-All-Time.

41 Bob Dylan, *Chronicles, Volume One* (New York: Simon & Schuster, 2004), p. 84.

42 Dan Roberts, "A Moment in Time," 1995, http://www.ehistory.com.

43 The Carter-Reagan Presidential Debate, October 28, 1980,
http://www.debates.org/index.php?page=october-28-1980-debate-transcript.
Interestingly, Reagan used the phrase "I think" twenty times.

44 Quoted in Tom Shales, "On TV, A Day That Speaks for Itself," *Washington Post*, January, 21, 2005, pp. C1, C9.
http://www.washingtonpost.com/wp-dyn/articles/A24730-2005Jan20.html

45 Eleanor Clift et al., "How Bush did it," *Newsweek*, November 15, 2004.

46 "The Persuaders," *Frontline*, PBS, November 2004,

Joseph J Romm

http://www.pbs.org/wgbh/pages/frontline/shows/
persuaders/themes/citizen.html.

47 Sigmund Freud, *Beyond the Pleasure Principle*, trans. James Strachey (New York: W. W. Norton & Company, 1961), p. 42.

48 Samuel Axon, "Lady Gaga first artist with one billion online video views," CNN, March 25, 2010, http://www.cnn.com/2010/SHOWBIZ/Music/03/24/lady.gaga.billion.video/index.html.

49 For a too exhaustive list of catch phrases, see http://www.tvacres.com/catch_coverpage.htm.

50 Stephan Lewandowsky et al., "Misinformation and Its Correction: Continued Influence and Successful Debiasing," *Psychological Science in the Public Interest*, 2012 in press; and Kimberlee Weaver et al., "Inferring the Popularity of an Opinion from Its Familiarity: A Repetitive Voice Can Sound Like a Chorus," *Journal of Personality and Social Psychology*, Volume 92, 821–833, http://www.apa.org/pubs/journals/releases/psp-925821.pdf.

51 Michael Deaver quoted in Bill Keller, "The Radical Presidency of George W. Bush," *New York Times Magazine*, January 26, 2003. http://www.nytimes.com/2003/01/26/magazine/the-radical-presidency-of-george-w-bush-reagan-s-son.html?pagewanted=all&src=pm.

52 Ann Richards' advisor (Mary Beth Rogers) quoted in James Fallows, "When George Meets John," *The Atlantic Monthly*, pp. 67-80. "President Participates in Social Security Conversation in New York," May 24, 2005.
http://georgewbush-whitehouse.archives.gov/news/releases/2005/05/20050524-3.html

53 Frank Luntz, "An Energy Policy for the 21st Century," *A New American Lexicon*, March 2005 (emphasis in original), http://www.politicalstrategy.org/archives/001207.php#1207.

Endnotes

"President Discusses Energy at National Small Business Conference," April 27, 2005.
http://georgewbush-whitehouse.archives.gov/news/releases/2005/04/20050427-3.html. John Carey, "Bush Is Blowing Smoke on Energy," *Business Week*, April 28, 2005.
http://www.businessweek.com/bwdaily/dnflash/apr2005/nf20050428_9012_db045.htm.

54 Mark Danner, "How Bush Really Won," *New York Review of Books*, January 13, 2005, pp. 48-53.
http://www.markdanner.com/articles/show/how_bush_really_won. In fact, Bush himself had repeated the line—the distortion—in his electioneering stump speech. For instance, in Orlando, Florida, on October 30, 2004, he said, "Americans need a president who doesn't think terrorism is 'a nuisance.'" As journalism professor Mark Danner, who attended the event reported, the woman next to him marveled that Kerry would say such a thing.

55 Dean Murphy, "If You Can Plug a Film, Why Not a Budget?" *New York Times*, February 13, 2005, http://www.nytimes.com/2005/02/13/fashion/13arno.html.

56 Margaret Wertheim, "Faith and Reason Website," http://www.pbs.org/faithandreason/theogloss/logos-body.html
Peacham, *The Garden of Eloquence*, from the "Epistle Dedicatorie."

57 The passage also reveals that Abraham was the godliest of men and Sodom the ungodliest of places, with not ten righteous men to save it from ruin

58 The 1992 speech can be found at http://www.nytimes.com/1992/07/17/news/their-own-words-transcript-speech-clinton-accepting-democratic-nomination.html?pagewanted=all&src=pm.
Clinton used the word "hope" in all its form, including his home town, Hope, eleven times.

The 1996 speech can be found at www.pbs.org/newshour/convention96/floor_speeches/clinton_8-29.html.

59 Howard Fineman, "Obama Puts Passion Into Jobs Speech Rarely Seen In His Presidency," September 8, 2011, *Huffington Post*,

http://www.huffingtonpost.com/howard-fineman/obama-jobs-speech_b_954874.html.

60 Transcript: Obama's Speech to Congress on Jobs, September 8, 2011, http://www.nytimes.com/2011/09/09/us/politics/09text-obama-jobs-speech.html?_r=1&pagewanted=all.

61 Frank Luntz, *The Language of Healthcare 2009*, May 2009. http://wonkroom.thinkprogress.org/wp-content/uploads/2009/05/frank-luntz-the-language-of-healthcare-2009l.pdf.

62 Matthew McGlone and Jessica Tofighbakhsh, "Birds of a feather flock conjointly (?): rhyme as reason in aphorisms," *Psychological Science Vol. 11*, September 2000, pp. 424–428.

63 James C. Humes, *Speak like Churchill, Stand like Lincoln* (Roseville CA : Prima Publishing, 2002), p. 115.

64 Carrie Chapman Catt, "Do You Know?" 1915, http://historynotes.net/2010/10/1915-do-you-know-by-carrie-chapman-catt.

65 Lincoln was inspired by the phrase "government of all, by all, for all," written over a decade earlier by Theodore Parker, a powerful Unitarian preacher who, in the 1850s, was heard by nearly three thousand people each week in Boston (almost 2 percent of the city's population). Dean Grodzins, *American Heretic* (Chapel Hill: University Of North Carolina Press, 2002), p. x.

66 Paul Tassi, "You Will Never Kill Piracy, and Piracy Will Never Kill You," *Forbes.com*, February 3, 2012. http://www.forbes.

Endnotes

com/sites/insertcoin/2012/02/03/you-will-never-kill-piracy-and-piracy-will-never-kill-you.

67 Maggie Haberman and Reid J. Epstein, "Decision day for Herman Cain," Politico, December 2, 2011, http://www.politico.com/news/stories/1211/69673.html.

68 Yale Project on Climate Change Communications, "Global Warming's Six Americas in May 2011," http://environment.yale.edu/climate/news/SixAmericasMay2011.

69 For a look of the latest science, see Joseph Romm, "It's 'Extremely Likely That at Least 74% of Observed Warming Since 1950' Was Manmade; It's 'Highly Likely' All of It Was," ClimateProgress, December 5, 2011. http://thinkprogress.org/?p=382209

70 Soren Kierkegaard, *The Concept of Irony* (Bloomington: Indiana University Press, 1965), p. 338. The full quote is, "As philosophers claim that no true philosophy is possible without doubt, by the same token, one may claim that no authentic human life is possible without irony."

71 The definition in the text is from *The American Heritage Dictionary of the English Language*, 4th edition (Boston: Houghton Mifflin, 2006), p. 924.

72 See J. A. Cuddon, *A Dictionary of Literary Terms* (Garden City, NY: Doubleday, 1977), pp. 329-334, and G. G. Sedgewick, *Of Irony*, (Toronto: University of Toronto Press, 1935, reprinted 1967), p. 10.

73 TV Quotes from "Columbo," TV Acres, http://www.tvacres.com/char_columbo.htm, and IMDb, http://www.imdb.com/character/ch0011637/quotes.

74 Churchill quoted in Thomas Montalbo, "Churchill: A Study in Oratory," *Finest Hour*, Fourth Quarter 1990, pp. 8-11, http://www.englishforums.com/English/AStudyInOratoryPartOne/gbnlp/post.htm.

75 James Fallows, "When George Meets John," *The Atlantic,* July/August 2004, p. 74.

76 Right after his re-election, Bush aides and friends began claiming that the true Bush is the mirror image of the "caricature" painted in the media of a stumbling, incoherent, non-reading, hands-off, if not just plain dumb candidate. On the contrary, they said, he is "a restless man who masters details and reads avidly," a man of "big ideas." Said one Republican senator in 2005, "When he calls you to talk about a bill, he knows the nitty-gritty."
Richard Wolffe, "Window of Opportunity," *Newsweek,* January 24, 2005.

77 The *Wall Street Journal* reported in 2005 that Bush's language changed noticeably after the re-election. In an address to European leaders in Brussels, "Mr. Bush spoke precisely, with only traces of his twang." He was pronouncing more 'ing' words without dropping the 'g' as he had been doing in 2004. His "more careful speaking style also has meant fewer verbal slip-ups." Bush paused more, so his speech appears more "considered," according to Stanford University linguistics professor Geoffrey Nunberg. John D. Mckinnon, "The Election Past, President's Message Gets a New Accent," *The Wall Street Journal,* March 21, 2005, page A1.

78 Churchill quoted in Humes, *Speak like Churchill, Stand like Lincoln,* p. 130.

79 Transcripts of the debates can be found at http://www.debates.org/pages/debtrans.html.

80 Holzer, *Lincoln at Cooper Union,* pp. 45-47. A campaign biography described him as "a man of the People, raised by his own genius and integrity from the humblest to the highest position." Holzer, p. 97.

81 Nicholas Kristof, "Crowning Prince George," *New York Times,* September 1, 2004.

Endnotes

82   Danner, "How Bush Really Won," p. 50.

83   Bush speeches available at http://georgewbush-whitehouse. archives.gov/news/releases/2004/11.

84   Danner, "How Bush Really Won," p. 51.

85   George Will, "Question time for Republicans," *Washington Post*, September 2, 2011, http://www.washingtonpost.com/ opinions/question-time-for-republicans/2011/09/01/ gIQAqpvexJ_story.html.

86   Thomas C. Peterson et al., "The myth of the 1970s global cooling scientific consensus," *Journal of the American Meteorological Society*, September 2008, pp. 1325-1337, http:// journals.ametsoc.org/doi/pdf/10.1175/2008BAMS2370.1. The study notes, "When the myth of the 1970s global cooling scare arises in contemporary discussion over climate change, it is most often in the form of citations not to the scientific literature, but to news media coverage."

87   Cuddon, *A Dictionary of Literary Terms*, pp. 329-334.

88   *Rhetorica Ad Herennium* (author unknown), tr. Harry Caplan (Cambridge: Harvard University Press, 1954), pp. 17-21.

89   The discussion of the Cooper Union speech is based on Holzer, *Lincoln at Cooper Union*.

90   Lincoln argues that beyond the twenty-one "fathers" who left an unambiguous voting record were "several of the noted antislavery men of those times" and ultimately defies "any man to show than any one of them ever, in his whole life," declared that he agreed with the original question. See Holzer, pp. 119-131.

91   Peter Wallsten, "GOP's election battle plan: Use Obama's own words against him," *Washington Post*, January 1, 2012. http://www.washingtonpost.com/politics/gops-battle-plan-against-obama-use-his-own-words-against-him/2011/12/30/ gIQA7ZrPUP_story.html.

92   H. L. Yelland et al., *A Handbook of Literary Terms* (Boston: The Writer, Inc, 1950), p. 180.

93   In Sophocles' *Oedipus Rex*, we know that Oedipus has, unwittingly, murdered his father, King Laius, and married his mother. The scenes in which Oedipus energetically pursues an investigation into the murder of Laius until its bitter end—even accusing the blind prophet Teiresias, who refuses to name the murderer, of keeping silent because he was an accomplice to the murder—are as ironic as any found in drama, which is why dramatic irony is also called Sophoclean irony.

94   Ann Althouse, "State of the Union versus *American Idol*," February 3, 2005, http://althouse.blogspot.com/2005/02/state-of-union-versus-american-idol.html.

95   "All-Time USA Box Office Leaders," http://www.filmsite.org/boxoffice.html. Note that this ranking is *unadjusted* for inflation (e.g. higher ticket prices) and rereleases. The top-grossing film of all time with adjustments is *Gone with the Wind*, a film with myriad ironies of its own.

96   Quotes from Anthony Leong, "Titanic Move Review," 1998, http://www.mediacircus.net/titanic.html.

97   Northrop Frye, *Anatomy of Criticism* (Princeton: Princeton University Press, 1957), p. 162.

98   Peacham, *The Garden of Eloquence,* p. 36.

99   *Othello,* John Andrews, ed. (London: J. M. Dent, 1995), p. 270. "Most modern scholars view John's revelations as a cyclical presentation of visions repeating, or recapitulating, the same basic message of present persecution, and the destruction of the wicked and reward of the just." Bernard McGinn, "Revelation," in *The Literary Guide to the Bible*, Robert Alter and Frank Kermode, eds. (Cambridge: Harvard University Press, 1987), p. 525.

Endnotes

100 "The 50 Greatest TV Shows of All Time," *TV Guide*, May 4, 2002, http://en.wikipedia.org/wiki/TV_Guide%27s_50_Greatest_TV_Shows_of_All_Time.

101 See, for instance, Jedidiah Purdy, *For Common Things* (New York: Vintage Books, 1999), pp. 9-11.

102 *Seinfeld* Episode Guide, Episode 59, "The Implant," http://www.tv.com/the-implant/episode/2299/trivia.html.

103 "Clinton Cheated 'Because I Could,'" *CBS Evening News*, June 17, 2004, http://www.cbsnews.com/stories/2004/06/17/eveningnews/main624309.shtml.

104 Jon Stewart, *Daily Show*, March 9, 2005.

105 Aphorisms Galore, http://www.ag.wastholm.net/aphorism/A-1233.

106 "For God speaketh once, yea twice, yet man perceiveth it not. In a dream, in a vision of the night, when deep sleep falleth upon men, in slumberings upon the bed; Then he openeth the ears of men, and sealeth their instruction." The book of *Job*.

107 See Steven A. Sloman, "Two Systems of Reasoning," in *Heuristics and Biases*, Thomas Gilovich, Dale Griffin, and Daniel Kahneman, eds. (Cambridge, UK: Cambridge University Press, 2002), pp. 385-386. See also Keith E. Stanovitch and Richard F. West, "Individual Differences in Reasoning: Implications for the Rationality Debate?" pp. 433-434.

108 Daniel Hamilton, "From Kinnock to Biden to Miliband," ConservativeHome, September 20, 2008 http://conservativehome.blogs.com/centreright/2008/09/from-kinnock-to.html.

109 "President Discusses Strengthening Social Security in Orlando, Florida," March 18, 2005,

http://georgewbush-whitehouse.archives.gov/news/releases/2005/03/20050318-9.html.

110 E. W. Bullinger, *Figures of Speech Used in the Bible* (London: Eyre and Spottiswoode, 1898), pp. 735-737. http://www.scribd.com/doc/10488338/Figures-Of-Speech-Used-In-The-Bible-Bullinger.

111 Diego Fernandez-Duque and Mark L. Johnson, "Attention metaphors: How metaphors guide the cognitive psychology of attention," *Cognitive Science, Vol. 23*, 1999, pp. 83-116.

112 Edward O. Wilson, *Biophilia* (Cambridge, MA: Harvard University Press, 1984), p. 60.

113 Daniel Kahneman and Shane Frederick, "Representativeness Revisited: Attribute Substitution in Intuitive Judgment," in *Heuristics and Biases*, p. 78.

114 Richard J. Harris, "Memory for Literary Metaphors," *Bulletin of the Psychnomics Society, Vol. 13*, April 1979, pp. 246-249 (cited in Gibbs, *The Poetics of Mind*, p. 133).

115 Ralph E. Reynolds, Robert M. Schwartz, "Relation of metaphoric processing to comprehension and memory." *Journal of Educational Psychology*, Vol. 75, June 1983, pp. 450-459.

116 *Rhetorica Ad Herennium*, p. 343.

117 Edward F. McQuarrie and David Glen Mick, "Figures of Rhetoric in Advertising Language," *Journal of Consumer Research*, March 1996. See also Anthony Greenwald and Clark Leavitt, "Audience Involvement in Advertising: Four Levels," *Journal of Consumer Research 11*, June, 1984, pp. 581-592.

118 "The Writings of Abraham Lincoln, Volume 2," page 37, available online at http://www.classic-literature.co.uk/american-authors/19th-century/abraham-lincoln/the-writings-of-abraham-lincoln-02/ebook-page-37.asp.

119 Churchill, "Scaffolding."

Endnotes

120 Jeffery Mio et al., "Presidential Leadership and Charisma: The effects of metaphor," *The Leadership Quarterly, Volume 16*, April 2005, pp. 287-294.

121 "How 2011 Became a 'Mind-Boggling' Year of Extreme Weather," *PBS NewsHour*, December 28, 2011, http://video. pbs.org/video/2181432528.

122 See "Parables, Similes and Metaphors," RE:Quest, http:// www.request.org.uk/main/bible/parables02.htm.

123 Paul Ryneski, "The All-Time Best Selling Singles," http:// www.neosoul.com/riaa/singles.html, and Russell Ash, "The Top 10 Selling Singles Of All Time—Worldwide," http:// www.jpgr.co.uk/stats_top10s_world.html.

124 "The Rolling Stones," http://en.wikipedia.org/wiki/The_ Rolling_Stones.

125 "The *Rolling Stone* 500 Greatest Songs of All Time," *Rolling Stone*, November 19, 2004,
http://www.scribd.com/doc/11793203/Rolling-Stone-500-Greatest-Songs-of-All-Time. See also, Geoff Boucher, "Honky Tonk Poet," *Smithsonian Magazine*, January 2003,
http://www.smithsonianmag.com/smithsonian/issues03/ jan03/tribute.html. Just the previous month, Dylan had been asked to sing a verse of Hank Williams' song "Lost Highway," which begins with the phrase as a metaphor: "I'm a rolling stone, I'm alone and lost/For a life of sin I've paid the cost."

126 *Webster's New International Dictionary Second Edition* (Springfield, MA: G. & C. Merriam Company, 1955), p. 1574.

127 Holzer, *Lincoln at Cooper*, pp. 123, 234.

128 Karen Tumulty, "Sarah Palin's 'blood libel' comment overshadows a calibrated message," *Washington Post*, January 12, 2011, http://www.washingtonpost.com/wp-dyn/content/ article/2011/01/12/AR2011011202145.html.

129 Chris Cillizza, "The Etch-a-Sketch incident and the art of the political gaffe," *Washington Post*, March 22, 2012, http://www.

washingtonpost.com/blogs/the-fix/post/the-etch-a-sketch-incident-and-why-some-gaffes-catch-on/2012/03/22/gIQA8ob0TS_blog.html.

130 Churchill, "Scaffolding."

131 Jocelyn Vena, "Lady Gaga Says 'Judas' Video 'Celebrates Faith,'" MTV.com, April 26, 2011, http://www.mtv.com/news/articles/1662707/lady-gaga-judas-music-video.jhtml.

132 Psalm 90 says, "The days of our years are threescore years and ten; and if by reason of strength they be fourscore years, yet is their strength labour and sorrow; for it is soon cut off, and we fly away." So Lincoln is making a biblical reference to the length of our lives by using the phrase "four score and seven years."

133 Basler, *A Touchstone for Greatness*, p. 80.

134 Kirkham, *English Grammar*, p. 223. The one example Kirkham cites is from Psalm 80, which has an extended metaphor of a growing vine: "Thou hast brought a vine out of Egypt: thou hast cast out the heathen, and planted it. Thou preparedst room before it, and didst cause it to take deep root, and it filled the land. The hills were covered with the shadow of it, and the boughs thereof were like the goodly cedars. She sent out her boughs unto the sea, and her branches unto the river." In my edition, Kirkham says this is the "60th" psalm, but that must be a typo.

135 See David Winston, "What Voters Want, The Politics of Personal Connection," *Policy Review*, June 1, 1999, No. 95, Heritage Foundation, http://www.hoover.org/publications/policy-review/article/7678. The TV ad directly connects to the widely used "life is a twenty-four-hour day" extended metaphor. For instance, part of Shakespeare's *Sonnet 73* describes a man who is in the *twilight* of his life.

Endnotes

136 See, for instance, "George Gipp," http://www.answers.com/topic/george-gipp.

137 See "Remarks at a Reagan-Bush Rally in Louisville," Kentucky, October 7, 1984, http://www.reagan.utexas.edu/archives/speeches/1984/100784b.htm. See also, "Remarks and a Question-and-Answer Session at Bolingbrook High School in Bolingbrook, Illinois," October 16, 1984, http://www.reagan.utexas.edu/archives/speeches/1984/101684b.htm.

138 George Lakoff and Mark Johnson, *Metaphors We Live By* (Chicago: The University Of Chicago Press, 1980), p. 3. See also *Metaphor: Implications and Applications* (Mahwah, NJ: Lawrence Erlbaum Associates, 1996), and George Lakoff and Mark Turner, *More Than Cool Reason* (Chicago: University Of Chicago Press: 1989).

139 Peacham, *The Garden of Eloquence*, "Epistle Dedicatorie." Churchill, "Scaffolding."

140 "Cyber Alert," September 13, 1996 (Vol. One; No. 75), Media Research Center, http://www.mrc.org/cyberalerts/1996/cyb19960913.asp.

141 Martin Lewis, "Unleash Hell On Al," time.com, November 05, 2000, http://www.martinlewis.com/column.pl?col=33&cat=time.

142 "Digging The Dirt," transcript, BBC-1, October, 22, 2000, http://news.bbc.co.uk/hi/english/static/audio_video/programmes/panorama/transcripts/transcript_22_10_00.txt.

143 Jim VandeHei reporting on *Morning Joe*, MSNBC, June 5, 2012.

144 NPR Weekend Edition, "Who Are Romney's Closest Advisers?" April 22, 2012, http://www.npr.org/2012/04/22/151146850/who-romney-keeps-close.

145 George Lakoff, *Don't Think of an Elephant* (White River Junction, VT: Chelsea Green Publishing, 2004), p. 73. George Lakoff and Mark Johnson, *Philosophy in the Flesh* (New York: Basic Books, 1999), p. 73.

146 Pierre Wack's quotes come from two articles, "Scenarios: Uncharted Waters Ahead," *Harvard Business Review*, September/October, 1985, pp. 73–89, and "Scenarios: Shooting the Rapids," *Harvard Business Review*, November/December 1985, pp. 139–150.

147 Steven Kull et al., "The Separate Realities of Bush and Kerry Supporters," Program on International Policy Attitudes, October 21, 2004, http://www.pipa.org/OnlineReports/Iraq/IraqRealities_Oct04/IraqRealitiesOct04rpt.pdf.

148 Fritz Wenzel, "Inside the Minds of Undecided Voters," an analysis of the Zogby/Williams Identity Poll conducted Aug. 11-16, 2004, http://www.puertorico-herald.org/issues/2004/vol8n38/38-Undecided.pdf.

149 E.J. Dionne, "Mass. Senate race's lesson for Obama," *Washington Post*, January 18, 2010, http://www.washingtonpost.com/wp-dyn/content/article/2010/01/17/AR2010011701934.html.

150 Ovid, "The Art of Love," in *The Erotic Poems*, tr. Peter Green (London: Penguin Books, 1982), p. 180.

151 Plato, *Gorgias*, tr. W. R. M. Lamb, http://www.lclark.edu/~ndsmith/sophists.htm.

152 Cicero, *De Inventione*, tr. H. M. Hubbell (Cambridge: Harvard University Press, 1949), p. 9.

153 Wayne A. Rebhorn, *The Emperor of Men's Minds* (Ithaca NY: Cornell University Press, 1995), p. 15.

154 Kevin Hogan, *The Science of Influence* (Hoboken: John Wiley & Sons, 2005), p. xii.

155 Peacham, *The Garden of Eloquence*.

Endnotes

156 Kevin Hogan, *The Psychology of Persuasion* (Gretna, LA: Pelican Publishing, 1996), pp. 85-89.

157 Paul Rozin and Carol Nemeroff, "Sympathetic Magical Thinking," in *Heuristics and Biases*, Gilovich et al. eds., p. 205.

158 Ian Skurnik et al., "How Warnings about False Claims Become Recommendations," *Journal of Consumer Research*, Vol. 31, March 2005, pp. 713-724. http://research.chicagobooth.edu/cdr/docs/FalseClaims_dpark.pdf

159 Seema Mehta, "Romney takes gentle swipe at Santorum at Iowa stop," *Los Angeles Times*, January 1, 2012.

160 Steve Rendall, "The 'Imminent' Argument," *Extra!*, March/April 2004, http://www.fair.org/index.php?page=1173.

161 David Sirota et al., "Center for American Progress responds," February 4, 2004. http://www.spinsanity.org/columns/20040205-cap.html

162 "In Their Own Words: Iraq's 'Imminent' Threat," Center for American Progress, Washington, DC, 2004, http://www.americanprogress.org/issues/kfiles/b24970.html.

163 U.S. Department of Defense, News Transcript, Tuesday, March 29, 2005,
http://www.defense.gov/transcripts/transcript.aspx?transcriptid=2548.

164 George W. Bush, "State of the Union," January 28, 2003,
http://www.washingtonpost.com/wp-srv/onpolitics/transcripts/bushtext_012803.html.

165 Maura Reynolds, "Bush Calls Iraq Imminent Threat," *L.A. Times*, January 29, 2003, http://articles.latimes.com/2003/jan/29/nation/na-bush29.

166 "In Their Own Words: Iraq's 'Imminent' Threat," Center for American Progress.

167 Mike Allen, "McClellan whacks Bush, White House," *Politico*, May 27, 2008,

http://www.politico.com/news/stories/0508/10649.html. McClellan wrote, "The collapse of the administration's rationales for war, which became apparent months after our invasion, should never have come as such a surprise."

168 Ian Skurnik et al. "How Warnings about False Claims Become Recommendations."

169 Shankar Vedantam, "Persistence of Myths Could Alter Public Policy Approach," *Washington Post* Staff Writer, Tuesday, September 4, 2007. http://www.washingtonpost.com/wp-dyn/content/article/2007/09/03/AR2007090300933.html

170 *Rhetorica Ad Herennium*, pp. 331, 403.

171 Peacham, *The Garden of Eloquence*, p. 118.

172 *Rhetorica Ad Herennium*, p. 321.

173 *Othello*, E. A. J. Honigmann, ed. (London: Arden Shakespeare, 2001), p. 37. All quotes from *Othello*, and all textual explanations [in brackets], in this chapter are from this edition.

174 Memorable Quotes from *Columbo*, "Ransom for a Dead Man," 1971, http://www.imdb.com/title/tt0066933/quotes.

175 Third Presidential Candidates' Debate, Arizona State University, Tempe, Arizona, October 13, 2004. http://www.debates.org/index.php?page=october-13-2004-debate-transcript

176 "Oh, Nevermind," American Idle, October 14, 2004. http://americanidle.org/wp/politics/oh_nevermind

177 Jonathan Swift, *Tale of a Tub*, http://etext.library.adelaide.edu.au/s/s97t/part5.html.

178 Vickers, *Classical Rhetoric in English Poetry*, p. 96.

179 Peacham, *The Garden of Eloquence*, pp. 27-29, pp. 196-198, pp. 180-181.

180 "High pitch, low politics," *The Economist*, March 23, 2005, http://economist.com/displaystory.cfm?story_id=3789210.

Endnotes

See also William Safire, "Dog whistle," *New York Times Magazine*, April 25, 2004, p. 38.

181 See David Greenberg, "Fathers and Sons: George W. Bush and his forebears," *The New Yorker*, July 12 & 19, 2004, http://agonist.org/node/2162/print. Bruce Lincoln, *Holy Terrors: Thinking about Religion after September* (Chicago: University of Chicago Press, 2002), pp. 19-32. Excerpted at http://www.press.uchicago.edu/Misc/Chicago/481921.html.

182 For the jester as Bob Dylan, see, for instance, P. O'Brien, "American Pie: The Analysis of the Song," March, 3, 1999, http://www.rareexception.com/Garden/Pie.php.

183 Dylan cited in Greil Marcus, *Like a Rolling Stone* (New York: Public Affairs, 2005), p. 33.

184 Shaheem Reid, "Lady Gaga Says Kanye West Saw Past Her 'Poker Face,'" MTV.com, May 6, 2009, http://www.mtv.com/news/articles/1610702/lady-gaga-kanye-west-saw-past-her-poker-face.jhtml.

185 "Poke Her Face," *Urban Dictionary*, http://poke-her-face.urbanup.com/4139436.

186 Cicero, *De Invention*, p. 3.

187 Wilson, *The Art of Rhetoric*, p. 48.

188 Ezra Klein, "Can you solve global warming without talking about global warming?" *Washington Post*, June 16, 2010, http://voices.washingtonpost.com/ezra-klein/2010/06/can_you_solve_global_warming_w.html

189 George Orwell, "Politics and the English Language," *Horizon*, Vol. 13, Issue 76, 1946, pp. 252-265, http://www.mtholyoke.edu/acad/intrel/orwell46.htm.

INDEX

211

Joseph J Romm

Index

17009455R00122

Made in the USA
Lexington, KY
21 August 2012